THE MACHIAVELLIAN'S GUIDE

GUIDE

TO

Charm

THE
MACHIAVELLIAN'S
GUIDE

TO
Charm

For Both Men and Women

Nick Casanova

iUniverse, Inc.
New York   Lincoln   Shanghai

THE MACHIAVELLIAN'S GUIDE TO CHARM
For Both Men and Women

iUniverse books may be ordered through booksellers or by contacting:

iUniverse
2021 Pine Lake Road, Suite 100
Lincoln, NE 68512
www.iuniverse.com
1-800-Authors (1-800-288-4677)

Because of the dynamic nature of the Internet, any Web addresses or links contained in this book may have changed since publication and may no longer be valid.

ISBN: 978-0-595-47237-6 (pbk)
ISBN: 978-0-595-70999-1 (cloth)
ISBN: 978-0-595-91519-4 (ebk)

Printed in the United States of America

To my mother, who would never stoop to using any of these tricks, but is still the most charming person I know

Contents

Introduction xiii

Part I   *Flattery*

"I'm Jealous" 3

His Age 5

His Intelligence 7

Set Him Up to Look Smart 9

Turn to Him for Advice 11

Praise His Wit 13

"You and I Have a Lot in Common" 14

"I Always Seem to Feel Good When I'm around You" 16

Cover His Ears 17

The Vague Compliment 19

Comparisons 21

"You Play Hardball!" 23

His Significant Other 24

His Children 25

His Dog 26

Let Him In on a Secret 28

Gentle Teasing 30

Pretend To Be Interviewing a Celebrity 32

When He's Been Gracious 34

Meeting and Greeting. 36

Introducing Your Prey 38

These May Sound Ridiculous to You, But Won't to Him 40

"That Moved Me" 42

"You're a Good Person" 44

"You Seem Like Such a Nice Person, But …". 46

"You're Way Too Smart to Be Making That Mistake" 48

Cancelling a Date. 50

"You're the Only Person I Know Who …". 52

For Richer 54

… Or Poorer 56

"Things To Do before I Die" 57

How to Escape 58

"You're So Charming" 59

"You're a Bad Influence on Me". 60

"What If I Hadn't Met You?". 61

Answering an Unanswerable Question 63

Scoff at His Insecurities 65

"Some Day …". 66

Part II   *Empathy*

Let Him Know You're More Nervous than He Is 71

If He's Just Been Fired 73

Be Sympathetic 75

"That's Really Tragic" 77

When He Commits a Faux Pas 79

"You're Too Sophisticated for Them" 81

If He's Worried about Being Weird 83

Don't Let Him Feel Alone 85

Hold the Door 87

"We're Having an Adventure" 89

Dynamic Duo 90

The Conspiratorial Wink 92

Pretend To Be a Nice Guy 94

Be Discreet 96

Quelling Jealousy 97

The Massage 99

Body Language 101

Part III   *Self-Deprecation*

Your Looks 105

Your Intelligence 107

If You're Fat 109

If You're Skinny 110

\ If You're Short 112

Your Job. 113

Summarize Your Occupation 115

Your Athletic Ability. 117

Your House 119

Your Car. 121

Your Clothes 123

"Men Are Such Pigs" 125

"Women Are Such Twits" 127

"I'm Nothing Special—Just Your Average Joe". 129

"I'm Inexperienced with Girls". 131

Be Racist against Yourself 133

Make Fun of Your Own Wimpiness. 135

If You Have a Reputation for Being Macho 137

2 Taking a Compliment 139

If He Looks at Your Photo Album 140

"I May Be Fat, But At Least I'm Slow" 142

"I Have No Self-Discipline" 143

"I Find Myself Quite Boring, To Be Honest" 145

If You're Second Choice. 147

If He Doesn't Remember You 149

Your Children 151

The Whispered Aside 152

"For Five Seconds There …" 154

When There's a Lull in the Conversation 156

"On the Internet …" 158

Part IV   *Recovering From a Faux Pas*

"I'm Shallow" 163

When You've Been Nasty 164

You're the Bad Guy 165

When Your Ego Shows 167

If You've Just Related an Accomplishment 169

"Thank You for Letting Me Boast" 171

If You've Been Caught Kissing Ass 172

When You've Been Stupid 174

If You've Overreacted 176

If You've Been Caught in a Lie 177

"I Don't Do Anything That's Not Calculated" 179

When You've Been Boring 181

When You've Repeated Yourself 182

If You're Caught Looking in the Mirror 183

The Greeting Kiss 184

If You Were Tongue-Tied 186

Part V   *Deference*

One Downmanship 191

"You're Like Catnip for Women!" 193

His Strength 195

2 "How Am I?" 197

"You're a Born Leader" 198

"You're the Alpha Male Around Here" 200

The Tough Guy 201

Flatter Him in the Most Sincere Way 203

"Someone Like You" 205

"I Hate People Who ..." 207

Talk about What a Lousy Lover You Are 208

"That's A Good Question" 210

"I'm Nobody" 211

Part VI   Being Cool

1 Roll With the Punches 215

2 "You Hurt My Feelings ..." 217

3 "That Doesn't Make Me a Bad Person" 218

A Stay Calm 219

Alcohol 221

Show Perspective 223

Don't Try Too Hard to Prove Your Masculinity 225

Agree with the Ridiculous 227

Don't Complain 229

If Your Prey Gets Something You Wanted 230

Keep It Clean 232

Afterword 233

Introduction

In the sixteenth century, Niccolo Machiavelli wrote a book, *The Prince*, about how to gain and keep political power through devious means. Since then, his name has become synonymous with dishonesty and evil. But using a touch of subterfuge in an effort to charm is not necessarily bad. Charm is, after all, mostly a way to make people feel good about themselves.

Charm can open many doors for you. It will help you progress in academia and get ahead in business. It will smooth relations with loved ones and land desired ones in bed. Charm makes people laugh and dissolves the tension inherent in just about any situation. It casts an enchanted spell on those exposed to it.

Luckily, charm is not so ethereal that it defies analysis. This book examines the individual components that comprise the magic: flattery, empathy, self-deprecation, and coolness. (Charm is the mirror image of obnoxiousness, which consists of being boastful, clueless, ham-handedly insulting, and often hysterical.)

The first section of this book is about flattery. Fashions come and go, but people will always want to be considered good-looking, successful, smart, athletic, and honorable (in that order). After a session with you, your prey should feel he is all those things. Your compliments needn't be true; they need only be plausible. The most effective flattery, of course, is that which seems unintended. This section will show you how to drop such "accidental" compliments.

Many of the suggested behaviors do not constitute charm in the classical sense: they will not make people marvel at your presence and wit. But they will make people feel better about themselves, and those people will then associate that feeling with you, which is the ultimate goal of being charming anyway. One of the secrets to being charming is to act charmed yourself. You must give someone your undivided attention and pretend to be impressed by him.

The next section is about empathy. Being empathetic means making your prey feel comfortable in any situation. Any points you score with a friend in need are basically worth double what you score at other times.

A naked, unadorned ego is a very ugly thing; the section on self-deprecation shows how to hide yours. If you can admit your weaknesses, people will consider you honest, perhaps even courageous. If you can actually laugh at yourself, people will instinctively sense they can trust you.

Another section is about deferring to your prey. It's a natural instinct to play one-upmanship. But charmers do the opposite and play one-downmanship—and then they pretend envy. This tactic combines both flattery and self-deprecation.

Charm often consists of doing the opposite of what our instincts compel us to: we must not only muzzle our own egos, we must act admiring as someone else's rages out of control. Nonetheless, our instincts get the better of us at times, and we slip up. The ability to recover from such a faux pas is vital. You can make any social error seem like a temporary slip rather than a permanent part of your personality if you acknowledge it. In fact, if you bounce back adroitly enough, you'll come across even better than had you never made the error in the first place.

The final section emphasizes how important it is to stay calm. Hysteria and charm are mutually exclusive. If you can stay cool when others succumb to anger or panic, you'll come across as heroic.

What gives flavor to this whole equation is, of course, the aplomb and the wit with which you do all these things. If you can act with flair, you will be irresistible. If you incorporate enough cleverness into your modesty and flattery, people will want to be around you just to see what comes out of your mouth next, and to see how you handle different situations.

With a real charmer, people will constantly marvel, "That was the perfect response—I would never have thought of that. He allowed the other guy to keep his dignity without losing his own, he stayed calm, and on top of that he managed to make everybody laugh." With enough practice, you can make people think this about you. And even if you do all these things without flair, you will still be likeable, which is infinitely better than being obnoxious.

There are sections of this book, and individual lines, that are slightly off-color. Choose what does and does not work given your personal style. And there are an infinite number of variations you can use on the themes of flattery, self-deprecation, and empathy. Be as creative as you like.

Above all, remember to keep your guard up: if you're charming some of the time and a jerk at other times, people won't like you. Being charming is a full-time job.

Many of the chapters are followed by examples of how a stiff, a boor, and a charmer would react in various situations. Most readers will identify with the stiff and recognize the boor. With practice, most stiffs will be able to transform themselves into charmers. The nature of boors being such as it is, they will remain boors even after reading this book—but that is poetic justice.

This book will refer to the person you are trying to charm as your "prey." This may sound overly aggressive, but do remember that, after all, you are trying to win him over with your predatory charm. And though the masculine pronoun is used for convenience's sake when referring to your prey, almost all the techniques work equally well with—and for—either sex.

The principles outlined herein are timeless. Hemlines may go up and down, but self-deprecation will always be in style and skillful flattery will always be appreciated.

PART I
Flattery

Abraham Lincoln once said that tact is the ability to describe others as they see themselves. Take this advice a step further: tell your prey he's better than he thinks he is. Having one's ego inflated is a heady experience, and if you can provide it on a consistent basis, your prey will eventually see you as the source of all things appealing and wonderful.

Your prey will be far more grateful about being praised for his weak points than his strengths. A champion wrestler does not need to be told what a good athlete he is; he will be infinitely more grateful if you tell him he's smart, or something else he rarely hears. Do make your compliments credible, for otherwise it will seem you're mocking him.

Remember that a compliment's value is in inverse proportion to the extent it sounds calculated: if you can flatter your prey without sounding as if that is your aim, all the better. Use these chapters as starting points, and then tailor them to his particular strengths and weaknesses.

① "I'm Jealous"

Nothing is more central to our self-image than our appearance. This can be proven by a simple test: when someone compliments you on your looks, don't you tend to remember it more than when someone tells you "nice job" for something you actually deserve credit for?

Above all else, you need to make your prey feel attractive. Direct compliments such as "You look nice" or "You're really good-looking" can sound a bit like everyday pleasantries. Pretending jealousy makes for a more memorable compliment.

"I'm jealous. If I looked like you, I'd have a new girlfriend every day."

"What did you ever do to deserve to be that handsome? Nobody deserves that."

"You must have been good in a previous life to get that face ... and I must have been bad."

Don't sound as if you're *trying* to give your prey a compliment; it will sound calculated and therefore less sincere. Sound as if you're truly jealous (but without the rancor) as you say, "Man, I wish I looked like you. Sometimes I think your looks are wasted on you."

"You're a handsome fool. If you had any idea how many women have had crushes on you!"

Even if your target is not attractive, you can usually find at least one feature that is praiseworthy. ("I wish I had an intelligent forehead like yours. I look like a cretin by comparison.")

These compliments work just as well for women, of course, with slight changes. ("If I looked like you, I'd just marry a billionaire.")

This "I'm jealous" formulation works well in conjunction with virtually every compliment: there's no feeling more sublime than knowing that you have sparked jealousy.

SITUATION: You catch your prey looking in the mirror. What do you say?

STIFF: Looks away quickly, as if he's caught him doing something shameful.

BOOR: "You gotta be the vainest guy I know."

CHARMER: (shrugging) "I don't blame you. If I looked like you, I'd probably allot an hour a day just to admire myself."

His Age

Women are, by reputation, extremely sensitive about their ages—but don't make the mistake of thinking that men are any less sensitive. So whether you're trying to charm a man or a woman, your job is to make your prey feel younger.

The rule of thumb when guessing somebody's age is that, up to the age of eighteen, you add a couple years, then, from eighteen to twenty-five you guess correctly. At thirty, you subtract five, past the age of forty you subtract ten, and from sixty-five on, you subtract fifteen.

Your prey is probably not such a fisherman that he'll ask you to guess his age. So when the subject comes up (e.g., when you see his driver's license, or when he mentions the year he graduated from college), just act surprised: "Oh, I thought you were younger."

Or say, "I guess you're younger biologically than chronologically."

Or just express disbelief: "No way you're forty-three." Then, add, "Wow! You're ancient," which, in context, is a roundabout compliment. Shake your head: "You're a medical miracle."

If your prey is thirtyish, ask, "Do you get carded when you go to bars?"

If you know you're the same age, comment, "It must be boring for you to hang out with an old coot like me."

If you're sure your prey doesn't dye his hair, accuse him of it. (You can be sure he doesn't if there are a few strands of white.) Likewise, if you're sure he hasn't had plastic surgery, examine his face closely and say, in a knowing tone, "You've had some work done, haven't you?" When he denies it, ask, "Then why don't you have any wrinkles?" When he shrugs, say accusingly, "Come on, tell me the truth." (As always, the best compliments seem unintentional.) When he says he is telling the truth, reply, "Then you're the luckiest person alive. You must never go out in the sun."

If your prey is literate enough to be familiar with *The Picture of Dorian Gray*, say, "You must have a picture in your attic that ages while you stay young."

Or, "You must have sold your soul to the Devil. What's it like having to do his bidding?"

Say, "You must be taking a human growth hormone or sheep's glands or something."

If you want to ask him about something he did earlier, don't ask, "What sport did you do when you were young?" This usage of the word "young" implies that he is no longer young. Ask instead, "… when you were a kid?" Not being a "kid" is far easier to digest.

Don't use the word "well-preserved"; it is usually applied to the very old, so implicitly assigns that age to your prey. And it evokes an ancient specimen pickled in a jar of formaldehyde, not the sexiest image. By all means, don't use this line with someone who looks older than his years, as if at one point he was left out in the desert to dry for a couple years.

SITUATION: Your prey tells you he's fifty.
STIFF: "Oh."
BOOR: "That all?"
CHARMER: "No way! What do you do, swim in the fountain of youth every day?"

His Intelligence ③

Tolstoy once said that although people never think they have a sufficient amount of money, everyone seems to think they have a sufficiency of intelligence. In fact, most of us think we're smarter than everyone else, since we agree with our own opinions more than anyone else's. Nonetheless, since we're all proven wrong from time to time, we harbor doubts, so we look for proof that we are indeed smarter than everyone else. (This is why we so enjoy those lists of dumb mistakes others make—they reassure us of our own intelligence.)

Tell your prey, "You're one of the smartest people I know." Virtually everybody in the top half—and bottom quarter—of the IQ bell curve is dumb enough to believe this.

If your prey demurs—probably insincerely—and lists his grades or SATs as proof, reply, "I'm not talking about that crap. I'm talking about real intelligence, you know, street smarts. You just seem to always be on target about people and stuff." Since virtually everyone believes in their own street smarts, he will accept your compliment at face value.

A roundabout way to make the point is, "You must think of most people as being really dumb."

When your prey says something *halfway* clever, exclaim, "I wish I had thought of that!" This always makes someone feel *very* clever.

No matter how banal his observation, marvel, "You're very insightful. As Sherlock Holmes once said, other people look, but you see."

It's okay if your prey ends up thinking you're a little dumb. To charm someone is not to overwhelm him with your superior smarts.

If you do all this, *you'll* end up feeling smart because of the ease with which you manipulated your prey. Just don't overdo it, or he may interpret your compliments as sarcasm.

SITUATION: Your prey confesses that his IQ was tested at ninety-three.

STIFF: Gives him an unintentionally disgusted look and shrugs.

BOOR: Nods as if longtime opinion has been confirmed and says, "That sounds about right."

CHARMER: "Well then, whatever it is that sets you apart can't be captured in an ordinary test."

Set Him Up to Look Smart

If your prey is not particularly intelligent, you can still make him feel as if he is. Ask questions you know he has the answer to, then act impressed with his response. He'll get that little zing of satisfaction for having known the answer, and you can reinforce his feeling of superiority by saying, "I had a feeling you'd know that," as if you consider him the ultimate source of all information.

Let's say your prey is a baseball nut. Ask him who won the World Series in 1986, and when he demonstrates his knowledge by telling you the Mets, try to look as happy as you would if your most cherished opinion about your own high intelligence has been confirmed. Exclaim, "I swear, you're a walking encyclopedia!" No matter that this encyclopedia begins and ends at B-a-s-e-b-a-l-l; look at him as if he has B-r-i-t-a-n-n-i-c-a stamped across his forehead.

Whatever random piece of trivia he happens to be in possession of, act as if he has just deciphered the Rosetta Stone.

If he's a crossword puzzle person, pick up a crossword yourself, stare at it in puzzlement, and say, "I don't get this. The clue is j-a-i and then there's a four-letter blank." When he tells you the answer is a-l-a-i, thank him and go back to the puzzle. Even if you can fill out a crossword without lifting your pen from the paper, stare at it in bafflement and continue to ask for help—on the easy answers. If he doesn't know the answer to a question, say, "I figured if anybody would know, it would be you."

Any error your prey makes is a mistake anyone could have made; if he gets something right, it's something very few people would have known.

Ask him about his field of expertise, whether it's geography or football or what it's like to be a twenty-year-old senior in high school.

Say, "Most people don't fully appreciate how smart you really are, do they?"

These comments work best with someone blinded by his own ego. (None of your comments should help him regain his vision.)

SITUATION: You ask your prey who his preferred candidate is in the upcoming Presidential election. He gives you his choice, but then adds that it's just another subjective political opinion, no better or worse than anyone else's.

STIFF: Nods.

BOOR: "That's true."

CHARMER: "See?! Just the fact that you would say that shows what good judgment you have!"

Turn to Him for Advice

You can make your prey feel both needed and smart if you ask him for advice. If the decision you're facing is a momentous one, all the better.

So whether you're trying to decide where to go to college, or which job to take, ask his opinion. No need to be subtle; spell out the flattery value of your question. Start by saying, "I've always thought of you as a valued ally, a trusted mentor. What do you think I should do?"

Or say, "Listen, I'm asking a few of the smart people I know their advice...." Then ask your prey which car to buy or where to rent an apartment.

Even if you consider your prey's judgment utterly worthless, ask anyway. Your prey gets to think himself the wise man of the village (even if he's the village idiot).

Then, if you happen to go with his suggestion (there's a 50 percent probability of this with an either/or decision), even though your decision wasn't influenced in the least by him, tell him that you took his advice: "I was going to take the job with Sears, but after talking to you I decided to go with Unilever instead." Let him think he changed the course of your life.

If you don't go with his advice, explain why, but tell him how his advice almost made you change your mind. He'll still glow.

You've got nothing to lose; you might even get some good advice.

SITUATION: You've made up your mind to marry Sally. Now you're sharing the news with your prey.

STIFF: "Sally and I are getting married."

BOOR: "I'm getting married. Lotta girls around here gonna be wearing black armbands."

CHARMER: "John—I've decided to ask Sally for her hand, but I didn't want to go ahead and actually do it till I got your blessing."

Praise His Wit

If you're not good at faking laughter, use words instead:

"I'll have to remember that one," as if you can't wait to repeat that particular gem.

"I could be your Boswell." Use this one only if he's literate enough to be familiar with the fellow who recorded Samuel Johnson's witticisms; most will think you're referring to the *Charlie's Angels* mentor.

"You could write for the movies."

"The ability to defuse tension with a joke is really a gift from God."

"Listening to you is sort of like being in a Noel Coward play."

"You could really do some damage if I were trying to keep a straight face at some solemn occasion."

To a third person, "I swear, this is the funniest guy I've ever met."

SITUATION: Your prey makes a weak attempt at wit.
STIFF: Manages a pained half-smile.
BOOR: "You are unbelievably lame."
CHARMER: "How do you come up with this stuff? Really, had you thought of that before and waited for the right moment, or did it just occur to you?"

"You and I Have a Lot in Common"

A roundabout but unmistakable way of telling your prey you like him is to tell him that the two of you have a lot in common. Nobody ever says that to someone he dislikes. In fact, people only say that to someone they like. Yet it doesn't sound like intentional flattery.

List the things you and your prey have in common. Say, "We both ran track, we both like the Beach Boys, and we're both interested in criminology." Say this with an air of joyful discovery; the hopeful note your prey should hear in the background is that this is the start of a long and beautiful friendship.

Commonalities of interest are preferable to institutional association. Better to both be interested in ornithology than to both be from Oregon—it's more incentive for future meetings.

Saying you have a lot in common means, on a very subtle level, that you *want* to be like this other person. This is somewhat akin to the way people always see their resemblance to better-looking, but never worse-looking, people. No one ever says, "Wow—we're so alike—we're both petty, vindictive, jealous people!"

Express pleased surprise at your "discovery" of your prey: "You know, I never expected to make a real friend in this place."

The feeling you want to give him is that each of you has just discovered his long lost twin.

One of the best ways to make your prey feel you have a lot in common is to pretend you are thinking what he is saying. So the next time he makes a casual observation, exclaim, "Wow! That's just what I was thinking!" He'll feel the kinship of like-minded souls, and he'll get that little zing of satisfaction one gets when credited for an astute observation.

At his next observation, cry out, "You always seem to say exactly what's on my mind!" Then give him a look of awe and wonderment, and say, "You know, we really think alike." (It's always reassuring, as well as fun, to meet someone who thinks the way you do.)

The next time, cry out, "You must be clairvoyant! This is amazing—it's as if you read my mind!"

Next time, "I'm starting to believe in ESP!"

A seemingly opposite—but in fact related—comment to make is, "Wow! I would never have thought of that!" When you phrase it like that, you're agreeing with his observation and saying you weren't smart enough to see it yourself. This is even more flattering.

Whether your prey is observing that the sun rises in the west or that the moon is made of green cheese, as long as he is your prey, agree with him emphatically.

SITUATION: Your prey says his favorite movie is *The Godfather.*
STIFF: "I've seen that."
BOOR: "Everybody in the world loves that stupid movie. Buncha Guinea gangsters. Who cares?"
CHARMER: (warmly) "That's one more thing we have in common! I love *The Godfather!*"

"I Always Seem to Feel Good When I'm around You"

The ability to bestow happiness is in fact a tremendous power, so telling your prey he makes you feel good is a tremendous compliment.

Another way to say this is, "I don't know why, but being around you always puts me in a good mood." (The "I don't know why" makes the compliment seem unintentional.)

Or, "Being around you always seems to take the edge off my bad mood."

"When I see you, I somehow just know I'm going to be enjoying myself."

Another way to say this is, "We always seem to have the most interesting conversations." The fact is, when you're talking about something you're really interested in, you're happy.

A more direct way to say it is, "You seem to be one of the few people who restore my faith in humanity."

SITUATION: After an enjoyable evening, your prey says, "That was fun."
STIFF: "It was."
BOOR: "I was in good form, wasn't I?"
CHARMER: "It's strange, but being around you is sort of like a drug—it just seems to give me this high."

16

Cover His Ears

When complimenting your prey to a third person, lightly place your hands over your prey's ears—you're only pretending you don't want him to hear. This will make it seem as if it is not your intention to flatter, which of course makes it even more flattering.

If your prey asks what you're doing when you place your hands over his ears, just reply, "I don't want your head getting too big."

The kind of flattery you deliver under these circumstances has to be somewhat sexy. It would be anticlimactic to place your hands over his ears, then just say, "John was a big help cleaning up after the storm." Much preferable to say something like, "John has all the local girls after him. If he had any idea how many of these girls are just crazy about him …"

If your prey is a woman, try, "Carla has no idea how often people talk about how beautiful she is." Even though she'll realize that your placing your hands over her ears is only a pretense, she'll still get that slightly illicit thrill that comes from hearing something one isn't supposed to. Afterward, ask, "Are your ears burning?"

If someone flatters you directly, there's a chance you'll write it off. After all, most flattery has an ulterior motive. But this approach, though somewhat transparent, still comes across as more sincere. Just be sure your prey isn't the type who'll feel he's had his personal space violated if you touch him.

The combination of having your ears and ego massaged at the same time is hard to resist.

SITUATION: Your prey, who is sitting in front of you, is being praised for his intelligence by a group of people. What do you say?

STIFF: Just nods.

BOOR: Slaps him on the back of the head like a reproving father and says, "If he's so smart, how come he's not rich?"

CHARMER: Covers his ears and says, "Don't you guys know how often he hears that? Everyone in the world knows how smart he is, if he hears it one more time his head won't be able to fit through that door."

The Vague Compliment

Human nature being what it is, if you give your prey a nonspecific compliment, he will happily flesh it out in his own mind.

Tell your prey, "You have a lot of animal magnetism." This is an intangible quality that has little to do with looks, and more to do with masculinity, and one that every guy, no matter how unattractive, is willing to believe he has.

Say, "You know, you're all right." Even if he's a sociopath (perhaps especially if he's one), he'll think, "Yeah, I really am all right ... I'm glad somebody else finally recognizes that." And he'll get that nice warm feeling inside.

Tell him, "You've really got your own sense of style, don't you?" Your prey may shrug and say, "I don't know, I guess so," but inside he'll be thinking: "Nobody else has a wardrobe just like mine, I guess I do have my own style." Or your prey may just interpret your comment to mean that he has his own unique personality. (Indeed, personalities are like snowflakes.)

Say, "You have a great sense of humor." Even if your prey is completely wit-free, he'll think, "He did hear me tell that joke about the traveling salesman the other day. I guess I am pretty witty."

Or give him that ultimate fill-in-the-blank compliment: "You really have something ... special." This your prey will probably swallow whole, for who among us does not feel special?

The vague compliment is sort of a Rorschach test that measures the self-delusional ability of your prey. Almost all men, and many women, will score high.

SITUATION: Your prey asks what it is about him that you like.
STIFF: "I don't know … You're a nice guy, I guess."
BOOR: "Nothing, really."
CHARMER: "It's hard to say … All I know is that you're one of a kind."

Comparisons

Comparisons are the form of flattery with the highest value: it's good to be good, but it's better to be better. As Gore Vidal once noted, "It is not enough to succeed; others must fail."

If Lauren is widely considered a beauty, what Julie would like to hear is not that she's "good-looking," but that she's "better-looking than Lauren." Beating others is a glorious victory; a compliment without reference points has less tangible value.

If your prey can point out some official award that so-and-so got that he didn't, pooh-pooh it: "Oh come on, that's just politics and you know it."

If your prey has an archenemy, comparing him favorably to that enemy will give him double satisfaction. ("Joe thinks he's some kind of genius, but he's not even close to being in your league.")

If no such enemies spring to mind, you can always use yourself as the benchmark: "You're about three levels above me in terms of intelligence."

But even winning a duel is not as satisfying as winning a championship, so the best way to stroke your prey is to use superlatives. Don't throw the superlatives around promiscuously. Be measured in your assessments of others, superlative in your praise of your prey:

Your prey is not a good skier, she's the best skier you've ever seen—and you used to watch your college ski team.

Your prey is not just "smart" (i.e., of slightly above average IQ). He's quite possibly the smartest person you've ever known.

And so on.

Plain vanilla compliments are boring. You want to come across like a shrewd, experienced horse trader who—after careful consideration—is convinced that your prey is the living reincarnation of Seattle Slew.

Just remember, if you're going to give your prey the Guinness treatment, there must be *some* credibility to your claims.

SITUATION: You've just witnessed your prey win a wrestling match.
STIFF: "Nice going."
BOOR: "Big deal. I know guys that could take you."
CHARMER: "It was sort of like a man against a boy. I guess that guy got a taste of what it's like to grapple against a real pro."

"You Play Hardball!"

You generally want to stay away from mean-spirited people—but if for some reason one of them is your prey, there's nothing to do but suck up and pretend that you're enjoying his cruelty. Telling him he knows how to enjoy himself is vague enough to be irrefutable. Sadly, for such a person, being mean *is* how he enjoys life.

The following lines, if said with the proper tone of amusement, will be construed as compliments by your nasty acquaintance.

"You don't pull any punches!"

"As Alice Roosevelt Longworth once said, 'If you don't have anything nice to say about anybody, sit next to me'!"

"Man! Now I know who to go to when I want the unvarnished truth!"

"That was the most I've laughed in ages!"

If he's mean about everybody, say, "You're like a great white shark—cruising around gnawing bites out of everyone."

Of course, if this person is not your prey, you want to get away from him as quickly as possible, *and* stay off his radar so you don't become a prime target yourself.

SITUATION: Your prey says about a mutual acquaintance that he is so fat he needs a bookmark to keep track of where his real chin is.
STIFF: Shocked silence.
BOOR: Laughs loudly and adds, "You're right! That pig never takes the feedbag off. I swear, just seeing him ruins my appetite."
CHARMER: Shakes head as if amused by the antics of a favorite but slightly naughty child, and says, "You *are* wicked!"

His Significant Other

Your choice of a spouse is the most important decision you will make in your life. Yet, even people who pay close attention to their choice of college and career will enter into a marriage for the flimsiest of reasons—namely, sexual attraction. Nonetheless, your spouse is a reflection on you, and you can make your prey feel good or bad depending on what you say about his.

Start by saying, "Wow, you got yourself quite a catch there."

Add, "You must be proud to be seen with her." You cannot say this if she isn't at least moderately attractive, otherwise it will be interpreted as sarcasm.

If even the scantest evidence of a brain is proffered, exclaim, "Wow, not only good-looking, but smart too!"

Add, "You must have beaten a lot of competition to get her. She could have had her pick." (*Not*, "You must have been the only guy who ever expressed an interest in her.")

If the subject of his wife's first marriage comes up, say, "Looks like she got it wrong the first time, right the second." (*Not*, "Whatsamatter? Couldn't get a new wife, had to get a used one?")

SITUATION: You've just met your prey's new bride.
STIFF: "It was nice to meet Susan."
BOOR: "Whenever you see a good-looking girl, you must regret marrying Susan."
CHARMER: "Looks like you're the winner in the marriage sweepstakes."

His Children

The best way to compliment your prey's children is to extrapolate from their current accomplishments to adult success. As ridiculous as this will sound to you, it's in the nature of parents to believe such nonsense.

So if you're informed that Billy Jr. got two base hits in his Little League game, nod sagely and say, "He could have major league potential in the long run." This is of course his parents' fondest dream, and such dreams usually preclude a realistic look at the odds.

If little Rebecca gets an A on a test, offer, "Who knows, a kid like that could end up as a Harvard professor, or even a Nobel laureate." The ludicrousness of this statement will be lost on the parents.

No matter what she looks like, you can exclaim, "She could be a child model!" (Parents are notoriously blind to their children's ugliness.)

If Johnny has a boyish cuteness (or even if he doesn't), say, "I can tell he's going to be a real lady killer. He'll probably break a lot of hearts." This will make any parent swell with pride.

If you're a parent, it's all too easy to get lost in a fantasy about your child's glorious future.

SITUATION: Your prey announces that little Bobby Jr. has a lemonade stand.
STIFF: "Oh."
BOOR: "Those things are so obnoxious. I never stop at them."
CHARMER: "He certainly has the entrepreneurial instinct. Sounds to me as if we have another Bill Gates on our hands."

His Dog

Complimenting your prey's dog is a great way to indirectly compliment him. It doesn't come across as if you're trying to flatter *him*, but you are. Start by kneeling down and giving the dog a good scratching. Dog owners assume that anyone who likes *their* dog must be nice.

Then, if it hasn't bitten you, say, "He seems like a good dog." Dog owners are generally about as objective about their dogs as parents are about their children, so he will undoubtedly be pleased that you see his dog's true nature.

Add, "He's certainly a handsome fellow. (You won't be contradicted; with dogs, the rule is, beauty is in the eye of the owner.)

If the dog obeys commands, observe, "Wow, he sure is a smart dog." Like parents, dog owners interpret the faintest sign of a working brain as evidence of genius, so he will agree.

If the dog is affectionate with your prey, say, "He sure seems to like you. He's well cared for, I can tell."

Ask if the dog was neutered. If the answer is yes, reply, "That's nice of you—you have to do that for his sake." If the answer is no, reply, "That's nice of you—too many dog owners just spay their dogs for their own convenience."

If your prey has a small dog, say, "I'm glad to see you're not one of those guys who feels it necessary to have a big attack dog in order to augment his masculinity." If he has a big dog, say, "Now that's a *real* dog! I hate those foofy little breeds."

If he feeds his dog leftover scraps from the table, point out, "That's nice of you to share your own food with your dog; most owners just give them dog food." If he doesn't, comment, "That's smart—you don't want to turn him into a beggar."

This line of talk will leave your prey basking in the warm glow of the knowledge that he is one of the good guys.

SITUATION: Your prey is out for a walk with his dog.

STIFF: Doesn't comment on it one way or the other, and shies away when the dog comes up for a sniff.

BOOR: "That thing reminds me of the mutt my sister used to have. We used to pelt it with snowballs. My sister would get so mad … What a bitch. Hey—that word describes both of them!"

CHARMER: "That's one lucky dog. You'd be surprised how many owners just leave their dogs tied up in the backyard all day long."

Let Him In on a Secret

Everybody likes being privy to secrets, and your prey is no exception. So let your prey in on a little secret from time to time. It will make him feel that he's part of your inner circle, a flattering place for anyone to be.

Most secrets aren't all that interesting, but if they're presented as "secrets" they seem to become more so.

First, swear your prey to silence, and make him promise on pain of death to never, ever tell *anyone*. (This usually insures that he will tell only two or three people.) Then, when telling your "secret," lower your voice, even if the two of you are standing on a deserted beach. (If you lower your voice, people will not only believe whatever it is you tell them, but will impute more value to it.)

If you don't have any secrets, just voice a long held suspicion. If you don't want to risk being wrong, just phrase it this way: "Don't tell anyone, but I'm pretty sure that ..." (It's always fun to speculate about who's gay, who's rich, who's cheating, who's an alcoholic, etc.)

Eventually, your prey will see you as a source of interesting information, and will value you as such.

SITUATION: Your prey is trying to ferret out some information from you about where Heather disappeared to for five months. You happen to know it was to a drug rehab clinic.

STIFF: "Uh ... I really shouldn't say."

BOOR: "None of your fucking business ... Anyway, if I told you, I'd have to kill you." Laughs at his unoriginal joke.

CHARMER: Says, "Can you keep a secret?" When prey says yes, Charmer asks, "No, I mean, can you *really* keep a secret?" When

---

prey says yes again, Charmer looks around to make sure no one else is listening, then tells him, "I think she has a secret boyfriend somewhere she doesn't want to tell us about."

Gentle Teasing

Gentle teasing is nothing more than a roundabout way of complimenting your prey's strengths. The key is to never address your prey's weaknesses, only his strengths. You should also be slightly overemphatic in your delivery to make sure he knows your intent.

Let's say you have a friend who's an excellent runner. One day he complains about how he was only able to run four miles at a six-minute pace that morning, as opposed to his usual five-forty-five pace. Respond, "Only six-minute pace? You should see a doctor!"

If your prey is rich, or at least richer than you, and complains about his money worries, offer, "If you like, we can pass the hat around for you."

You get the idea.

Ask your Greek God of a friend, "How can you stand to be *so* fat?"

To a tough guy, "You're *such* a wimp."

If your prey complains that women don't like him, name the ones who do, then comment, "I guess *they* don't like you either."

This type of gentle teasing is welcome whenever your prey puts himself down, but, in keeping with the friend-in-need theory, is even more welcome when he has been criticized by someone else. If your runner friend is told by someone else, "I'm about as fast as you," after that person is gone, repeat, sarcastically, "He's *every* bit as fast as you, you know."

Whenever your prey puts himself down, exaggerate his comment to make it look silly.

SITUATION: Your prey, fishing for a compliment, says he could only bench press two hundred and forty pounds that day.
STIFF: "That doesn't seem so bad."
BOOR: "I know guys who can bench four hundred."
CHARMER: "You're *so* weak—I'm surprised you can lift your fork and knife."

Pretend To Be Interviewing a Celebrity

If your prey does something creditworthy, instead of just praising him, take it one step further and pretend that he's famous for his exploit. If he gets the impression that you're mocking him, you must stop. But if he realizes you're just playing a friendly game, you can both have fun with this.

Start by holding up an imaginary microphone and saying, "Are you the John Smith who scored a one hundred on his math exam?"

"To what do you attribute your great success?"

"At what point did you know that you had the exam aced?"

"Does the pressure of being a role model ever get to you?"

"Any words of advice for all your fans out there?"

"I guess someone in your position has to be very careful of what he says, in case it gets misconstrued."

"Were you born in a log cabin, or a manger?"

Whatever his response, ask, "Is that on or off the record?"

"Are you worried about kidnapping or assassination? How many bodyguards do you normally travel with?"

"In my wildest dreams, I never thought I'd get an exclusive with John Smith! What a scoop! Listen, would it be unseemly if I asked for your autograph?"

SITUATION: Your prey shot a hole-in-one at his golf course the previous weekend.
STIFF: "Nice going."
BOOR: "Why don't you tell someone who cares."
CHARMER: (holding up an imaginary microphone) "Mike Smith, UPI. Sir, is there any truth to the rumor that steroids helped you accomplish this feat?"

When He's Been Gracious

Gracious people are forever bothered that their graciousness passes unappreciated, or even worse, unnoticed. It's your job to let your prey know that his actions are not taken for granted. So if he's nice to you, respond:

"You're way too kind."

"It's so nice to be with someone who's so well-mannered."

"You're such a skillful flatterer you always manage to make me feel as if I'm a better person when I'm around you."

"You're so nice. Sometimes I think you're too nice for your own good."

"You're one of the most generous people I know."

"You are the soul of benevolence."

"You always say the right thing, don't you? I honestly have never seen you make a wrong move."

"You must have been brought up well, to always be so courteous."

"You're an angel."

Your gracious prey will undoubtedly say something gracious back; comment on this as well. Go ahead and turn it into an out-gracing competition—one of the few virtuous activities that actually *is* its own reward.

SITUATION: Your prey has just given painstakingly detailed directions to a stranger from out of town.
STIFF: Says nothing.
BOOR: "It's more fun to give the wrong directions."

CHARMER: (shaking head in wonderment) "I don't think most people appreciate how gracious you really are."

Meeting and Greeting

Your opinion of your prey is almost always communicated in the first five seconds after seeing him. If you blow these first five seconds, you are reduced to spending the rest of your time with your prey trying to undo the message your body language conveyed.

The first thing you must do is look pleased to see him. This is the hardest thing to fake, but also the most important. A cold, impassive stare will send a chill down his spine and pretty much negate any subsequent friendliness.

The next thing is to call out his name heartily. If you can't remember his name, try to avoid saying, "Sorry, I'm drawing a blank on your name," which usually means that he barely registers on your radar screen. Instead, just say, "*Heyyyyy!*" with extra enthusiasm, and add, "I was just thinking of you!"

Then shake his hand heartily, and give him the double handclasp, grasping the back of his right hand with your left; this conveys twice the enthusiasm. Then, before letting go with your right hand, clasp his right shoulder with your left hand.

The impression your greeting should leave him with is, "Gee, I didn't know he liked me that much."

SITUATION: You see your prey approaching you in a hallway.
STIFF: Holds up one hand as if to stop him and says, "Hi ...," uncertain whether it's appropriate to stop and chat, starting an awkward pas a deux.
BOOR: Says "What's up?" in the tired voice one uses when expecting to be hit up for the latest of a long series of favors.

CHARMER: Approaches him squarely so he must stop, pumps his hand excitedly, and says, "Hey! I was *hoping* I would run into you."

Introducing Your Prey

This is one of the best opportunities to flatter your prey. Start by telling the third party, "This is the guy I was telling you about, the one who's such a good golfer." This way you not only work the compliment in, you inform your prey that he's important enough to you that you've actually been telling others about him.

You can communicate the same thought even more strongly by saying, "Here he is, finally, in the flesh—John Smith!" The implication here is that you've been going on at length about him.

Or, after introducing your prey, tell him, "You've been heavily advertised to Bill here as the coolest guy in the world—so don't disappoint him!" On the surface, your act is kiddingly confrontational, but the underlying message is that you've been building him up.

Or say, "This is the guy I was saying is so funny." Turn to your prey. "You have a big rep to live up to, I hope you're feeling witty today."

Or say to the third party, "I know you've been wanting to meet him." This will make your prey feel important, and it will probably dawn on him that the only reason the other guy would want to meet him is because you've been building him up.

It is preferable to have said something about your prey to the third party; if your comment is met by a blank stare, your credibility may suffer.

SITUATION: You're introducing your prey (John Smith) to a third party.

STIFF: "Rob, this is John."

BOOR: Doesn't bother to introduce them.

CHARMER: "Rob Callahan, meet John Smith—yes, THE John Smith."

These May Sound Ridiculous to You, But Won't to Him

The following lines—or at least variations on them—can be uttered on any occasion. They seem a little far-fetched, and therefore must be delivered without even a hint of sarcasm, but if your prey has a typical ego, he'll eat them right up.

If you've just been watching him in action, try one of these:

"It's been a real privilege to watch you play tennis."

"What a treat it is to hear you play the piano."

If you've actually been competing against him:

"It's been an honor just to be on the same court as you."

"I really don't feel worthy to play tennis with someone as good as you."

"You always bring out my best—you're an inspiration to me."

The following are all-purpose lines that can be trotted out on any occasion:

"It's always a special occasion just to be in the same room as you."

"I know it sounds silly, but I feel as if your presence somehow elevates me."

"I feel as if I'm in the presence of greatness. I really do."

"It's not often I get to be around someone like you."

"I have so much respect for what you stand for." If he asks you what that is, answer as if you're surprised that he would even ask: "Integrity and intelligence, of course." (Everyone believes they have these two qualities.)

"I feel I'm a better person for having known you."

"I feel like I ought to genuflect in your presence."

If you ever retreat in an argument, just say, "I always defer to my superiors." (Don't say this if he is actually ranked ahead of you in an organization, since that gives the statement a different meaning.)

You have to be a real BS artist to deliver these lines with a straight face, let alone the conviction they require, but if you've practiced enough of the other techniques in this book, you probably qualify.

SITUATION: Your prey appears at a restaurant you own.
STIFF: "Hi John."
BOOR: "Oh, you again."
CHARMER: "John, you honor us with your presence. This is now hallowed ground."

"That Moved Me"

If your prey tells a personal story with strong emotional content, for instance an inspirational story about a dead relative, he's expecting more than a noncommittal shrug and look of boredom afterward. It is incumbent upon you to offer an emotional response. You needn't burst into a torrent of tears, but you should say something along the following lines:

"That touched something in my soul."

"That stirred me. It really did."

It's a fine line between such statements and sarcasm; you must take great care to walk this side of it, by being firm but not overly emphatic, and by maintaining eye contact.

Or, just stare at him for a few seconds, as if speechless, then say, "Wow." (Sometimes just silence will speak more eloquently.)

Or, "You think I'm going to cry, but I'm not." Then open your eyes wide as if struggling against it. (This is an indirect way of letting your prey know he has achieved the desired effect.)

Don't be afraid to wipe away an imaginary tear. (Your prey will never know it wasn't real.) Even as a subconscious gesture, it states what your prey wants to hear. If you can manage to sound choked up, even better. If you can actually produce real tears, best of all.

SITUATION: Your prey has just told you about his mother, whom he had been embarrassed to have to push around in a wheelchair when he was young, but who was so proud of him, and how after she died, he was so ashamed of the fact that he had been embarrassed by her.

STIFF: "Oh."

BOOR: "Yeah, I can see why you'd be embarrassed by a mother in a wheelchair."

CHARMER: "That's an amazing story." Shakes his head thoughtfully.

"You're a Good Person"

While describing someone as "nice" is often seen as a weak substitute for more substantive praise, people in fact like to be reassured that they are decent human beings. So when the opportunity arises, tell your prey that he's a good person.

"You're really a decent person, aren't you? I can always tell, I'm a good judge of these things." This will both flatter your prey and cause him to believe that you actually do have good judgment.

"You really do have a strong moral compass, don't you? I can tell by the way you always refrain from the kind of selfishness most guys indulge in."

"You're one of the few people who's really guided by his conscience. You have all the signs: you're generous, you're unfailingly polite, you always seem to do the right thing."

"I can tell you were brought up well because you're never nosy."

"Only a good person like you takes such great care to be diplomatic all the time and not hurt anybody's feelings."

"You're very good about sharing credit, aren't you. That's very generous of you." (It's nice to be thought of as "generous" without having to actually part with any money.)

"If there is a heaven, you're one of the people who's going."

SITUATION: Your prey has just finished talking to a couple of very elderly people.
STIFF: Makes no comment.
BOOR: "What are you wasting your time with those dried up old raisins for?"

CHARMER: "I can tell what a good person you are by the way you're so solicitous of people from whom you have nothing to gain."

"You Seem Like Such a Nice Person, But …"

Once you've established what a good person someone is, you can actually use that as leverage to get your way. Tell your prey, "You seem like such a nice person, and yet you won't even give me those front row seats." The implication is that the only thing that prevents him from attaining full "nice person" status is giving you those desired seats.

It's a way of gently cajoling your prey into giving you what you want, while complimenting him at the same time. It's gentle because you've told him you think he's nice, except for this one little thing. Many people will immediately think, "I *am* a nice person, and this guy realizes it." Now, most people aren't going to take you all that seriously, and, if pressed, would say that you were just tossing off a meaningless line, but at a certain level, they'll still react positively and will want to remove that one blemish from their otherwise perfect reputation.

Use it to obtain whatever you want:

"You seem nice, and you probably come from a nice family, so why are you being so mean to me?"

"Up till now I would have said you were a decent person, the type who would be susceptible to embarrassment and shame, yet here you are trying to cadge money off me."

When your prey finally bends to your demands, give him the positive reinforcement he deserves: "There—I *knew* you were a good person."

SITUATION: A waiter at a fancy restaurant seats you next to the kitchen.
STIFF: "Would it be possible to get another table?"
BOOR: "Hey, don't be an asshole. We don't want to sit here."
CHARMER: "You seem like such a nice person, yet you're putting us way off in Siberia."

"You're Way Too Smart to Be Making That Mistake"

If you want to correct your prey, or change his behavior, but also want to keep him in a receptive frame of mind, it's best to combine your advice with the above piece of flattery. In fact, if you phrase it this way, people will accept just about any correction.

On balance, the positive overall view of their intelligence you are suggesting will outweigh the one small mistake they're making, and they'll gladly admit an error in exchange for this flattery. In fact, they'll probably have such a positive view of your judgment—for rating their intelligence highly—that they will *want* to believe you're right, and will fall all over themselves accepting your suggestion.

Contrast this to the response you'll get if you start out by calling them stupid: a mulish obstinacy that will not admit fault no matter what.

So try any of the following lead-ups to a criticism:

"You know better than that …"

"I'm surprised that somebody as smart as you would be capable of making a mistake like that …"

"A brilliant guy like you thinks that? Now I've seen everything …"

"Come on, use that big brain of yours …" (Be careful this doesn't come across as sarcasm.)

"You're the first guy I've ever met with an IQ over one-fifty who thinks that …"

"Well, I guess even supercomputers make errors …"

"Sometimes I think you're so smart that your brain is taken up with such weighty topics and it doesn't have time to think about such small, insignificant matters like this ..."

"No one as smart as you should ever fall for that ..."

Or, "No way someone with your brains should be letting that guy outsmart you ..."

SITUATION: Your prey says that the capital of Japan is Hong Kong.
STIFF: "No, it's Tokyo."
BOOR: "*Jesus Christ* are you an idiot! It's Tokyo!"
CHARMER: "Come on, someone as smart as you knows it's Tokyo. You just had a slip; you must be tired."

Cancelling a Date

If you don't want to do something with your prey, rule number one is, lie. Your excuse must be something unavoidable—and something you'd obviously rather not be doing. It can't be, "Joey has some extra Rolling Stones tickets and I'd rather go with him."

Rule number two is, you must also make it sound as if you're merely postponing, not canceling, which has a much harsher feel to it. Always ask for a "rain check."

Rule number three: express regret—not for your prey, but for yourself. A good way to do this is, "I'm so disappointed. I had really been looking forward to this. You know, I think I would have enjoyed the picnic even more than you would have." This is flattering, and also sounds sincere.

Rule number four: "try" to reschedule. If there are times or dates when you know he's busy, try to reschedule for those dates. When he tells you he's unavailable, express frustration.

Rule number five: let this frustration turn into anger at whoever or whatever caused your withdrawal (before any actual rescheduling can take place). Erupt in fury: "I'm so angry. I can't believe I have to go!" Or, "That goddamn Joey. He's always screwing things up!" (If your prey is trying to reschedule, your fury should cause him to lose his train of thought.)

Rule number six: don't express any guilt, because guilt is something you would feel only if you were purposely standing your prey up, and you don't want to leave that impression.

Rule number seven: ask him to do something you know he doesn't want to do. "At least promise me you'll come to my daughter's piano recital tomorrow night."

You want to leave him with the impression that he has somehow rejected you, not the other way around.

SITUATION: You want to cancel your dinner plans with your (same sex) prey because you've got a hot date.

STIFF: "Listen, would it be okay if I cancelled our dinner? I finally got Sherri to go out with me."

BOOR: Simply doesn't show up.

CHARMER: "Can I take a rain check on dinner? I'm really sorry, but I'd forgotten I'd promised my mother I'd take her to her bingo game tonight. Hey—do you want to come?"

"You're the Only Person I Know Who …"

We all like to think ourselves unique. On the other hand, we tend to regard others as interchangeable, and we sense that they regard us the same way. Therefore, any evidence that others *do* see us as unique is always welcome. You can provide this welcome evidence to your prey by telling him, "You're one of a kind. You're the only person I know who …"

What follows should be some kind of compliment, preferably pointing out what a polymath he is:

"… knows both world history and sports."

"… can change a tire and recite poetry."

"… can both iron a shirt and shoot a gun."

There's got to be some combination that makes your prey unique. Think about it, and have the compliment prepared for the next time you see him.

The compliment need not necessarily be a twofer, though; a single will suffice, as long as it's flattering enough:

"… is so effective with difficult personalities."

"… can charm such a wide variety of people."

"… has the courage to go bungee jumping."

SITUATION: Your prey has a bad case of attention deficit disorder, and hops from one subject to the next.
STIFF: Does his best to follow the conversation.
BOOR: "Will you stick to the subject for Crissakes?"
CHARMER: "You're the only person I know who, in the space of five minutes, can segue from explaining stock market psychology to cracking a funny joke to talking knowledgeably about crime statistics. A true Renaissance man."

For Richer …

If your prey is rich, equate his money with power, success, and even sexual desirability (sadly enough, this is mostly true). Encourage his belief (common among the rich) that money is everything.

Let's say your prey is worth half a million dollars. Tell him, "You know, the median household net worth in this country is thirty thousand dollars. That means you're over sixteen times as successful as the average household!" (Your prey would much prefer to think of himself this way than as the poorest guy at his investment bank.)

"You could have all sorts of servants working for you if you wanted. You could have people doing your bidding night and day."

"It's got to be great not to have to worry about money." If your prey says he does worry, tell him, "If you worry about money with the amount that you have, then you're a jerk." (This sounds like an insult, but the underlying message is, hey, you're rich, so don't worry; that's what will stick with him.) Add, "Seriously, what worries do you have? Paying for your great-grandchildren's education?"

"If I had your bank account, I'd be livin' large."

"Tell me—those people who say money can't buy happiness—they're wrong, aren't they?"

"Let's face it. There's only one way to measure success in this country, and you've achieved it."

Call your prey Moneybags, Croesus, Midas, or Bill Gates Jr.

Do anything but compare him to people who have more money than he does; that will drive him crazy.

SITUATION: Your prey boasts that he is now finally a millionaire.
STIFF: "Congratulations."
BOOR: "That's nothing these days."
CHARMER: "I'm a little worried about you—can you fit through the eye of a needle?"

… Or Poorer

If your prey is poor, take the opposite approach and denigrate the values of Mammon.

If he has kids, say, "There's only one way to measure wealth, and that's by the children you have."

"Our society is too money-oriented. If you have a roof over your head and food to eat, that's all you need. These people with four houses are so silly—you can only sleep in one house at a time."

Point out a rich person and say, "He has poverty of the soul."

"What counts in life is whether you've helped other people."

"What do rich people do other than sit around and count their money all day long?"

"Your kids are lucky in a way that they're not too rich. Look how screwed up rich kids are. Look how many of them commit suicide."

"Hey, if you're rich, you never really know if people like you for yourself or if they like you for your money. If you're poor, at least you know who your friends are. The Beatles were right—you can't buy love, that's for sure."

Of course, this is mostly nonsense, but it's nonsense geared towards making your prey feel better about himself, so go ahead and spout it.

SITUATION: Your prey bewails the fact that he doesn't have as much money as a mutual acquaintance.
STIFF: "Oh well."
BOOR: "No two ways about it, being poor has gotta suck."
CHARMER: "I bet he'd give all his money to look like you. Or to be as young as you."

"Things To Do before I Die"

If you happen to have a paper and pencil handy when your prey (Joe) happens by, write in large block letters, "List of Things To Do before I Die" across the top of the paper, so that he can't miss it. Then create a list. For example:

1. Climb Everest
2. Publish a Book
3. Make a Million Dollars

Draw his attention to what you're writing by whatever means necessary.

Then, ostentatiously write down your last goal:

4. Become Better Friends with Joe

He should be amused by what is obviously a joke, but also flattered since it may have a grain of truth to it.

Then purse your lips and judiciously say, "At the moment, I can't tell which is going to be harder to accomplish, number one or number four ... probably number four."

If he's clever, he may respond, "I tell you what, I'll become better friends with you as soon as you climb Everest."

To which you should reply, "That's a deal. I'll start making arrangements for my trip tomorrow."

How to Escape

There are times when you really want to get away from someone, especially if you're at a party with other people you'd rather be talking to. The trick is to accomplish that without communicating how you feel.

One way is, "It's been really great talking to you." If you say this with enough enthusiasm, the person you're talking to may not even realize that you're purposely drawing the conversation to an end. Follow this up with, "Be sure to say good-bye before you leave," then take his hand and shake it with both of yours, as if you really want to see him again.

Another tactic is to say, "Oh, there's someone I want to introduce you to," if you spot someone with any common interests. Call the other person over, introduce them, then at least you'll have someone more interesting to talk to as well. If you manage the situation skillfully, you can actually take your leave and stick the new person with the boring one.

Or say, "Oh no, there's Zeke, and I promised I'd talk to him about his dissertation. I've been dreading this, but ... oh well, wish me luck." This sounds as if you're being dragged away against your will.

SITUATION: You're at a cocktail party, stuck talking to someone you want to get away from.
STIFF: "Sorry, but I have to go talk to Jerry about something."
BOOR: Walks away without saying anything.
CHARMER: "I'd love to stay and chat, but I'm afraid my wife will kill me if I don't pay attention to her." Shrugs and looks heavenward in despair.

"You're So Charming"

One of the best ways to charm is to convince your prey that he's charming. (Even if he is a boor—perhaps especially if he is a boor—he'll believe you.) So point this out.

"You always seem to say just the right thing."

"You always know what to say, don't you?"

"You have more good lines than anyone else I know."

"You can charm anyone …"

Shake your head and grin, "… the birds right out of the trees."

Or, "… the pants right off of anyone." (The sexual connotation here is acceptable given that it is a common expression.)

"Whatever it is you have, if you could bottle it, you could make a lot of money."

"You can probably get people to do you a lot of favors, can't you?"

"It's too bad there aren't more people like you. If everyone were as charming as you, all wars would stop and we could all live in peace."

"It's as if you read a book on how to be charming, and you memorized it. Heck, you could *write* a book about charm."

As always, envy drives the compliment home: "I wish I were as charming as you."

SITUATION: Your prey has been the life of a party, and a friend of his points this out. What do you say?

STIFF: (nothing)

BOOR: "I don't think so."

CHARMER: "What's it like, having the entire world wrapped around your little finger?"

59

"You're a Bad Influence on Me"

If you do anything out of character while with your prey, attribute it to his influence. Whether your actions are laudable or naughty, if you give him credit for them, he'll be flattered that he has an effect on you:

"I wouldn't have done that before I met you."

"See? That's the kind of effect you're having on me."

"It's entirely your fault." (In the right context, this is a compliment, especially if used after a commendable action.)

"Thanks to you, I now seem to be a new person."

"Now you've got me [doing this]."

"You know how after watching a Bond movie you find yourself talking like Sean Connery? You seem to have that same effect on me."

"Is hanging out with you what's known as 'falling in with a bad crowd'? Because I can feel myself being brought over to the dark side a little more each time I see you." (Say this only if he prides himself on his naughtiness.)

SITUATION: Your prey suggests a second beer, one above your normal limit.

STIFF: "No thanks. I was planning to run five miles this evening."

BOOR: "Long as you're paying."

CHARMER: "You are definitely a corrupting influence on me. Now you've got me drinking to excess. I really do seem to be under your sway."

"What If I Hadn't Met You?"

One of the best ways to underline your appreciation of your prey is to say how lucky you feel to have met him:

"What a stroke of luck to be in the same course as you!"

"When I think, if I hadn't just happened to have the seat next to you in that airplane, we never would have met!" Shake your head as if that would have been a tragedy almost on par with the plane having crashed.

"You know, I think it was fate for us to meet like this. We just have too much in common *not* to have met." (This is of course ridiculous, but it expresses the same feeling.)

"You know, I remember seeing you across the cafeteria a couple times, and I have to admit, I never would have guessed that we would end up becoming such good friends."

"You never know what kind of people you're going to meet any place you go. Believe me, I've met every type, and how wonderful it was to meet someone so intelligent and decent here."

"It's really strange when you think about the role that luck, or circumstance, plays in peoples' lives. We all have a story to tell—most of our parents met by chance, really, when you think about it. And when you think about the way you were conceived, if that particular sperm cell hadn't happened to fertilize the egg—you would have been your brother or sister—or somebody else. And then, when I think of how I just happened to meet you …" Shake your head in an "ah, the wonder of it all" way; the message that you're happy you met your prey will be clear.

SITUATION: Your prey happens to mention the circumstances of your meeting.

STIFF: Nods.

BOOR: "That was your lucky day."

CHARMER: "It actually scares me to think that if either of us had decided not to go to that party, none of this would ever have happened!"

Answering an Unanswerable Question

Unanswerable questions fall into two basic categories: compliments and insults. The best way to respond to both is with a self-deprecating comment that will either tickle or mollify your prey.

Complimentary questions are those such as, "How did you ever get to be so funny?" or "When did you get so cute?" or "Is there anyone else in the world nearly as smart as you?"

One way to respond to these is to say, "You seem to think I'm something more than I am. But misguidedly high opinions of me are always welcome."

Another way to deal with such questions is to say, "I have to disagree with the premise of your question."

Negative unanswerable questions, on the other hand, tend to call for more individualized responses:

If someone cries out, "When are you going to grow up?" purse your lips as if seriously pondering your answer, then reply, "Probably never. You know, my middle name is Peter Pan."

If someone says, "Will you get lost?" answer in a child's voice, "But there's nowhere else I'd rather be."

If someone asks, "Will you get out of here?" answer, "I'm starting to get the sense—call it a hunch—that you don't want me here."

If someone asks, "What makes you so stupid?" reply, "That's a question I've pondered long and hard, but I haven't been able to come up with a satisfactory answer yet—probably because I'm so stupid."

The idea behind these comments is not to just defang your opponent, but to make it clear with a lighthearted reply that you're not bothered by his insults either. When viewed in this light, it becomes clear that no question is totally unanswerable.

SITUATION: Your prey asks, in a fit of anger, "Why are you such a pain in the ass?"

STIFF: Pulls back as if stung by a bee, but can think of nothing to say.

BOOR: "You fucking asshole, I oughta beat the shit outa you!"

CHARMER: (shrugging) "Because it's so much fun!"

Scoff at His Insecurities

When your prey gives voice to genuine self-doubt, scoff with ill-concealed disgust at the very notion that he could harbor such silly thoughts.

If he says he's dumb, cry out, "What? You can't be serious! You're smarter than 90 percent of the guys who come through here! The only thing you're lacking is confidence."

In fact, any cliché, if uttered with scathing enough contempt for the thought he's expressing, will work. Remember to follow up with the suggestion that he has the quality he feels he lacks—in abundance—and then the statement that all he lacks is confidence.

By reassuring your prey this way, you will earn his undying gratitude. Remember, these are not just lines to be recited woodenly. You need to muster as much contempt for his statement of self-doubt as you possibly can into your tone of voice. The more scathing the contempt, the more the compliment is worth.

SITUATION: Your prey says he doesn't think he's very tough.
STIFF: "Oh well, toughness isn't that important."
BOOR: "That's always been my impression."
CHARMER: "Are you fishing for a compliment here? Because if you are, forget it. You know perfectly well how tough you are."

"Some Day …"

Another way to assuage your prey's insecurities is to paint a picture of his glorious future, based on whatever quality he feels he does not have.

If he worries about his career as an academic, say, "After they give you the Nobel Prize for Biology, just remember that I was the first one to spot your promise."

If he expresses worry about his ability to make the high school baseball team, say, "I *know* you're going to make it. In fact, after you get drafted by the major leagues, I'll be expecting you to get me some box seats at your stadium."

If he says he has no future in politics, say, "I have a feeling that some day you're going to be elected president. And when you do, I'll be expecting you to make me the secretary of state."

If he bemoans his lack of ability to get girls to go out with him, say, "Some day, they're going to be breaking down your door. And when they are, I want you to remember me, and funnel some of your rejects my way."

If he worries that his career as an actor is going nowhere, say, "I have a feeling you're going to make it. And when you win your Oscar, I'll be expecting thanks in your acceptance speech."

By combining your prediction with a somewhat selfish statement—that you want to be remembered somehow—it will add a touch of credibility to your statement about his fantasy coming true. And even if he knows that these are just pleasant fantasies, the fact is, they *are* pleasant, and he will associate that feeling with you.

SITUATION: Your prey says he'll never be a success in business.

STIFF: "Well, success is a relative term."

BOOR: "Yeah—but you've got a great future as a cashier at McDonalds."

CHARMER: "When you become a billionaire and have all sorts of courtiers fawning all over you, I want you to remember that *I* was the one who told you you'd be rich—and I want you to remember me—in your will."

PART II
Empathy

Flattery is what people want, but empathy is what they sometimes need. If you can provide this, you will become indispensable. Your prey will be impressed that you understand his travails, grateful that you consoled him, and touched that you made the effort.

Keep in mind, empathy is not the same quality as sympathy. Empathy is the ability to imagine what others are thinking and feeling; sympathy is the expression of concern for another's plight. In order to effectively sympathize, one must be able to empathize. Then, of course, you must be able to express that sympathy without sounding condescending. Even better than that is to console your prey without him fully realizing what you've done.

Let Him Know You're More Nervous than He Is

People can be phobic about athletic events, musical recitals, college tests, public speaking, flying, all sorts of things. Whatever it is that causes your prey's stomach to turn over, let him know he's not alone. Nothing calms a nervous person down more than knowing that others are even more nervous.

Let's say you and your prey both have to give speeches, and you know that he has a public speaking phobia. Even if you're totally blasé about speaking in public, confide in him that you're extremely nervous.

Tell him, "I have a really bad case of butterflies in my stomach. I'm so nervous, I'm afraid I may throw up in the middle of my speech."

Look at your palms, then wipe them on your pants. In case he doesn't get the point, say, "My palms are sweating."

By now your prey should be feeling a little better. If he's not, use a little humor. Examine your crotch closely. When he asks you what you're doing, reply, "I'm waiting for the little dark spot to appear." Add, "Listen, if I crap in my pants don't tell anyone, okay?"

Shake your head and say, "I could sure use a drink right now. Actually, I could use about three. Or maybe a tranquilizer—maybe one of those hypodermic darts they shoot into the rhinos to calm them down before they check their teeth on the nature shows."

Shakily say, "I'd rather have root canal work done than have to do this."

If your prey still seems nervous, say, "Actually, I'd rather die. I wish I were dead right now." The ridiculousness of this statement should put his fear into perspective.

After your prey's speech is over, if he asks you, "Were you really that nervous? You sure didn't seem nervous when you gave *your* speech," admit, "Well, maybe I was exaggerating a little. But didn't it make you feel better?" (There's no point in doing anything you're not going to get credit for.)

Anyway, you don't want people thinking that you're some kind of Nervous Nellie.

SITUATION: You and your prey are both about to compete in your college conference championships, and he says he's extremely nervous.

STIFF: "You'll do fine, I think."

BOOR: "You're such a woman. Grow a pair of balls, willya?"

CHARMER: Replies, "You?!" Takes a deep breath and puts a finger on the inside of his wrist, then looks at his watch. Announces, "*My* heart rate is a hundred and forty. God I hate this feeling. I hate it, I hate it, I *hate* it."

If He's Just Been Fired

Losing one's job is supposed to be the third most traumatic experience one can have (behind the death of a loved one and a divorce). So if your prey has just lost his, you can score friend-in-need points by consoling him.

Turn the firing into a roundabout compliment: "They didn't like you because you're too strong. You're not just a yes-man."

"You're one of the few people who can leave that place with his head held high. You never became an ass-kisser or a backstabber."

"You were too good for that job. They resented you because they knew you were smarter than them."

Put it into perspective: "It's just a job. They say the average person has sixteen jobs in his lifetime, and switches careers three times."

"I read once that over 70 percent of people who lose their jobs are making more money within a year and a half than they were before they lost their job."

"I didn't want to tell you this before, but that guy you worked for seemed like a real jerk." (Your prey will hardly be in a frame of mind to disagree with this.)

Thoughts of revenge are always sweet. "Maybe we could put a pipe bomb under his car."

If you're absolutely sure he won't take it, offer to lend him some money to tide him over.

SITUATION: Your prey has just lost his job.

STIFF: "That's too bad."

BOOR: "Maggie's not going to go out with you anymore if you don't have any money."

CHARMER: "Ten years from now you'll probably walk back in there and buy the place."

Be Sympathetic

No matter how little sympathy your prey deserves, pretending to feel some for him as he suffers—or as he imagines he suffers—will pay dividends.

It's not hard to figure out what he wants to hear. If he shows you his injury, it's for one reason only: he wants you to fret and cluck over it. Indulge him.

Your average guy wants to feel like the hero in the movies who brushes off your concern and gets to look tough as a result.

Let's say he has a hangnail. Wince and exclaim, "Ouch! That looks painful." Increase the level of sympathy for more serious injuries accordingly.

People want sympathy for their stressful lives as well. So listen to your prey with a straight face—even if he's a drama queen whose average day is filled with one "dire emergency" after another.

Cluck, "I know how you feel," and "I don't blame you for feeling that way," even if all you feel is contempt.

Or murmur, "I'd have a hard time dealing with that too," even if you can barely believe the tempest-in-a-teapot nature of his problems. People like this want to feel like victims, even if their problems are all of their own making. Let them.

Whatever you do, don't break out laughing.

When it comes to charm, honesty is rarely the best policy, and it can be the worst. ("That's all you're upset about? I thought it was something serious.")

SITUATION: Your prey took a fall while playing soccer and sustained a bruise, which he shows you.

STIFF: "Oh."

BOOR: (laughs as if it's funny) "Relax, you'll survive. Jesus, you're such a baby."

CHARMER: "If that happened to me, I wouldn't have been able to keep playing."

"That's Really Tragic"

If your prey has had a recent downturn in his fortune, one way to make him feel better is to laughingly exaggerate the dismal nature of his misfortune. You have a fine line to walk here: there are times when he wants sympathy; in those instances, refer to the previous chapter. But there are other times when what he needs is to have his common sense jump-started.

Let's say he just got turned down by a girl and is feeling blue about it. Any of the following lines, delivered with a touch of sarcasm, will do the trick:

"How long are you going to be in mourning about this?"

"That's really too bad, because, you know, she *is* the last girl left on earth."

"I'd been feeling bad about [a recent disaster that caused great loss of life], but now I guess I have something to *really* feel bad about."

"I'm certainly glad you're not the type to make a mountain out of a molehill."

"I think I hear violins playing in the background."

Or you can take a more direct approach. Just say, "Snap out of it, will you? You're embarrassing yourself. You may not realize it now, but you will in a couple days. And worse, you're embarrassing me."

Or try, "I'm just curious. How do you plan to react when something really tragic happens?"

Forcing someone to gain perspective is not an unalloyed plus for your relationship, but on balance it goes into the plus column, especially if it allows him to feel better about his "plight."

SITUATION: Your prey has just gotten a D on a test, bringing his overall grade for the course down to a B-. He seems to be overreacting.

STIFF: "That's too bad."

BOOR: "Ha! Serves you right for being such a weenie."

CHARMER: "I haven't had a really good cry in a while. This will give me the opportunity. About time my tear ducts got cleaned out."

When He Commits a Faux Pas

If your prey commits a social error, he'll probably realize it, and a friendly word pooh-poohing the error would be welcome. (If he doesn't realize it, it's best not to inform him of his error. After a guest once drank from his finger bowl, Queen Victoria was reputed to have done likewise, in an effort to keep him from realizing his error.)

If your prey embarrasses himself publicly, whisper to him that this particular group doesn't approve of that particular behavior, that they're a little weird that way. Chuckle, "Billy, for some strange reason, around here people think it's wrong to pat a woman's ass if you don't know her, so you might want to hold off on that while you're in town."

Or act as if he's a rare treasure who keeps you constantly amused and awed at his originality: "Billy, I've got to hand it to you, there aren't many guys who'd take a leak on the street in full view of everybody."

Or give your prey absolution on the grounds that he's a bold, straight-talker who tells it like it is: "The problem with the world today is that there's not enough honesty. Now that that lady knows she has a fat rear end, she may go on a diet, and she'll be better off, thanks to you."

Or laud your prey as a dispenser of rough justice, the type of fellow who likes to see wrongs righted: "That guy'll sure think twice the next time he tries to hail a cab in front of somebody else. I'll never forget his expression when he saw you had smeared mustard all over the back of his coat."

These examples of behavior may be a little extreme, and people who commit them are unlikely to be susceptible to embarrassment. But for most of us, even lesser actions would result in a very red face. If you can lighten that tint just a shade on your prey, you will ingratiate yourself.

SITUATION: Your prey unintentionally but audibly passes gas at a party.

STIFF: Looks disgusted and steps away.

BOOR: (loudly, drawing the attention of even those who had not noticed it) "Oh, you pig! Peee-uuu!"

CHARMER: (*sotto voce*, to prey) "We all get gas. It's not as if anyone here never let one rip before."

"You're Too Sophisticated for Them"

If your prey prides himself on his wit, but doesn't get the recognition he feels he deserves, tell him what he wants to hear: that it's his audience's fault:

"You're too sophisticated for them. They couldn't appreciate you even if they wanted to."

"You're wasted on this crowd. You need a more intelligent audience."

"This bunch would be better served with Roadrunner cartoons."

"If you acted like one of the guys from *Dumb and Dumberer,* they'd be in hysterics."

With enough of this pearls-before-swine talk, you'll have your prey convinced he is the reincarnation of Mark Twain.

This type of compliment actually applies to all sorts of situations: Your prey should be in a better school ("You're wasted here.") He should be working for a better company ("They're lucky to have you—they don't even realize how talented you are.") He deserves a better girlfriend ("You could have your pick—she doesn't appreciate what she's got.") And so on. Never mind that what you say isn't true; the compliments are vague enough so as to be hard to refute. (Luckily, few people are leery of these types of blandishments.)

SITUATION: Your prey has just spent the evening in a vain attempt to get a few laughs from his dinner table companions.

STIFF: "Oh well."

BOOR: "That went over like a lead balloon. You better keep your day job."

CHARMER: (whispers to prey) "Having you here is like sticking Cary Grant in a Three Stooges movie."

If He's Worried about Being Weird

A common teenage ailment—even more so than acne—is to worry about being considered "weird," especially since teenagers frequently accuse each other of this. If your prey is worried about this, you must convince him he is normal.

Start by saying, "You're weird? What's weird about you? Do you haunt houses? Do you turn into a werewolf at night? Or do you just have the kind of kinky sexual fantasies everybody has, but no one admits to?"

"Guess what? It's the most normal thing in the world to worry about not being normal. In fact, the fact that you worry *proves* you're normal. The really weird people are sociopaths, who never worry about not being normal. You're obviously not one of them."

Continue, "You seem pretty normal to me." (Go on long enough, and he'll soon be trying to prove he's not boringly normal.)

Ask, "What do you want to be normal for, anyway? Normal is boring. Anyway, we're all weird in our own way."

"By the way, do you know what the definition of a normal person is? It's someone you don't know very well."

Sarcasm works here: Name a few things he does that are slightly offbeat, then say, "You're *so* weird. No one's *ever* done those before."

Conclude with the following speech. "You know why some people think you're weird? Because you're smarter than they are. They can't relate to you because your IQ is thirty points higher than theirs. They don't even get your jokes half the time, so they call you weird because they don't want to feel dumb. When you start to meet more people as smart as you, believe me, you'll feel normal."

SITUATION: Someone calls your prey weird for collecting stamps, then walks away.

STIFF: Looks at prey, and makes no comment.

BOOR: Laughs harshly, "He's right."

CHARMER: "Half the kids on my block had a stamp album when I was growing up. Anyway, have you ever noticed it's always the people who accuse others of being weird who are in fact the weirdest?"

Don't Let Him Feel Alone

You're never lonelier than when you're in a crowd you don't fit in with. So if your prey is obviously out of place somewhere, even if you fit in, tell him you've always felt a little out of place there, and his own sense of alienation will be eased.

The two of you are at a piano recital. Everyone else looks blissfully appreciative, but you can tell your prey is bored out of his mind. Even if everybody else is just faking it, your prey's trapped feeling will be exacerbated if he thinks he's the only one who feels that way. So whisper in his ear, "Is this hell? Or is it just purgatory?"

You're at a funeral and everybody is carrying on about what a wonderful guy the deceased was. You, however, know he was a skunk, and you happen to know your prey feels the same way. Whisper to your prey, "I have to check who's in that coffin, because from the way people are talking, I don't think it's actually [the deceased]."

You're with a group of athletes and your prey is the only non-athlete present. Even if you're six feet six inches and two hundred and fifty pounds of lean muscle mass, whisper to him that you've never really felt at home with a bunch of dumb jocks.

No matter the situation, no matter the subject, guys in groups are particularly susceptible to groupthink, or at the very least, groupspeak. Your prey may feel the only way he can belong is through such lip service. If you let him know you feel the same way he does, he will then belong—without lip service—to a group of two.

The more intelligent your prey, the fewer groups he'll feel at home with. If you let him know he's not alone, he will ever after feel a certain kinship with you.

SITUATION: You and your prey are listening to your coach give a pre-game pep talk, which he ends with a rousing cry to "kill" the opposing team.

STIFF: Raises his fist and weakly says, "Yeah."

BOOR: Stands up, pumps both fists, and yells, "Kill! KILL RIDGE-FIELD!!" at the top of his lungs.

CHARMER: Raises one fist and whispers to prey, "What a bunch of morons."

Hold the Door

Certain basic good manners are a prerequisite to charm; Emily Post devoted an entire book just to manners. And it is true that everyone likes to feel pampered, as if the other person's consciousness is completely attuned to their comfort. It makes them feel important. This seems obvious, but it works, so it must be mentioned.

Many think that most of these niceties apply only to men with women: offering her your jacket if she's cold, lighting her cigarette, walking on the outside of the sidewalk, and so on. But in fact they can be used by either sex, with either sex; your aim needn't necessarily be sexual seduction.

Refill your prey's wineglass (it's always nice to have someone else "force" you to get tipsy).

If your prey drops something, immediately pick it up before he has a chance to bend over himself.

If you're a guest, help clear the table and wash the dishes afterward. Make your bed. Help with all chores, the more unpleasant the better.

Offer to help carry your prey's bags. Offer to carry anything heavy.

Any small sacrifice you can make, make, and afterward say, "It's nothing."

Offer your prey a ride anywhere he's going.

Acting as if you were brought up well implies good character. So if you have good character, advertise it with your good manners. If you have bad character, all the more important to cover it up with faultless manners.

SITUATION: You and your prey arrive at your car.

STIFF: Uses his remote to unlock both doors, gets in on his side.

BOOR: Uses the key to unlock his own door, gets in, starts the car, puts it in reverse, then, only as an afterthought, steps on the brake and reaches over to unlock his prey's door.

CHARMER: Walks to the passenger side door, opens it, and holds it open for his prey. When his prey is comfortably seated, he closes the door firmly but gently, and only then goes around and gets in himself.

"We're Having an Adventure"

We all grew up reading about Tom Sawyer, or Nancy Drew, or Tarzan. But none of *us* lead lives nearly as exciting. There's actually a way to turn your prey's humdrum life into an adventure. And that is by simply telling him it is so. (Often by describing something a certain way, it becomes perceived that way.)

If your prey seems bored, tell him, "You're approaching this with the wrong attitude. You think going to the drug store to have your prescription filled is just another tedious chore to slog through. But it's not. We're having an adventure. Who knows what could happen on the way? We could stumble across a satchel with a million in untraceable bills inside. We could even get kidnapped and held for ransom. Hey—our lives are *fraught with peril*."

If you're just watching a movie, nudge your prey and point out, "Hey, the great thing about seeing a movie is that we get to experience the adventures without putting our own lives at risk. It's great, isn't it?"

The best thing about this approach is, by cheerfully spouting such nonsense, you'll actually improve your own attitude.

SITUATION: You and your prey are on your way to a party, hoping to meet some girls.
STIFF: "I hope there aren't too many guys there."
BOOR: "Girls there better not be a buncha skanks, like that last party you took me to."
CHARMER: "The night is young, anything could happen. And you know what? There's no one I'd rather share this adventure with. Because whenever I'm with you, for some reason the world just seems like a more appealing place."

Dynamic Duo

The most effective way to tell your prey you feel close to him is to let him know that he is half of a unit of two—the most exclusive club in the world.

Say, "I rarely feel this way, but I feel like I'm undergoing a real male bonding experience with you."

"We make a great team."

"We're partners in crime."

"We should have a secret handshake or something. Or have a little ceremony where we become blood brothers."

"Here we are—the Dynamic Duo."

"I never expected to make such a good friend at my age."

"You're one of my best friends." (Don't worry that he doesn't consider you his best friend, he'll still be flattered.)

"I hope we're friends for a long time."

"This is going to sound awfully corny, but I really feel like we're … soul mates."

"I feel like Tom Sawyer with Huck Finn."

If you think you can pull it off, sing "Moon River": "Two drifters, off to see the world … There's such a lot of world to see …"

If there are three of you present, refer to "The Three Musketeers … one for all and all for one."

Some of these lines can make you sound somewhat pathetic, but they should also make your prey feel warm inside.

SITUATION: The subject of friendship arises during a discussion between you and your prey.
STIFF: "I consider you a friend, I guess."
BOOR: "I figure it's every man for himself."
CHARMER: "I feel closer to you than I feel to anyone else outside my family, and that includes my girlfriend."

The Conspiratorial Wink

Nothing quite spells C-H-A-R-M like a friendly, humorous wink. It says, "You and I are in this together" and "Don't take this too seriously" and "I've got things under control" and "We're having a good time" all at the same time.

Think of the people you've known who've had the presence of mind to be able to wink at you during a stressful situation. Were any of them not charming?

Winks are great for defusing tension. Let's say you've gotten into a violent argument in front of your prey. When the person you're arguing with looks away for a moment, turn to your prey and give him a quick wink. This shows that you're not really taking the argument too seriously, and that even though you sound angry, to a certain extent you're just playacting. It also shows that your prey is the one whose opinion you care about, since you've taken the trouble to wink at him.

The wink can also reduce your prey's anxiety. Let's say he's about to play a piano concerto in front of an audience and is very nervous about it. Tell him, "You'll be great, I just know it," and wink at him. The wink indicates that you have complete confidence in him, which helps make him feel confident in himself. (If this doesn't loosen him up at all, a playful shove can do the trick.)

A wink is also a great way to temper a boast. Let's say you've just bellowed, "I am the greatest of all time," or some variation thereof. (Muhammad Ali merely gave voice to what most of us secretly feel.) If you give a playful wink to your prey right afterward, it sends the message that you're just fooling around, that you don't really take yourself all that seriously. It makes it seem almost as if you said it just to make fun of yourself. (Ali gave this impression as well, which explains his popularity.)

SITUATION: The car in front of you stops suddenly, and despite the fact that you slam on your brakes, you still hit it. The other driver gets out, and after a quick glance at his rear fender, comes up and yells, "What the hell do you think you're doing?"
STIFF: At first, says, "Oh shit." Then, when the other driver walks up angrily, responds, "Sorry."
BOOR: At first, yells, "Goddamn it!" Then yells at the other driver, "It was your fault, you fucking asshole! Why did you stop like that?!"
CHARMER: After asking his prey if he's okay, he then winks at him and says, "I don't think I'm about to become fast friends with this guy."

Pretend To Be a Nice Guy

One of the ways that serial killer Ted Bundy evaded suspicion at first was to act like a nice guy. He even worked at a suicide hotline, the kind of thing you do only if you really want to help people (or, like Bundy, really want to savor their pain).

You, like Bundy, can fool your prey into thinking you're nicer than you are.

While you're out with your prey, hand a homeless person a dollar. This will prove your Nice Guy bona fides more effectively than if you handed your prey a hundred dollar bill (he would simply wonder why you're trying to buy him). Yet by giving one hundredth of that amount to a homeless person from whom you have nothing to gain, you've achieved Nice Guy status. (In finance, this is known as leverage.)

Don't say anything afterward. It's easy to ruin the effect by pontificating about how you like to help the less fortunate, or there but for the grace of God, or some such blather.

If you're at a party, take your leave of a good-looking woman by saying, "My mother always taught me that a man should spend as much time talking to the unattractive women as he does to the beauties, so I'm afraid I'm going to have to work my way around the room a bit more." Add, "I *do* plan to come back for some more dessert later on though."

Get a dog. Dog lovers tend to have affectionate dispositions and don't mind caring for others or even cleaning up their messes. (You can be sure Ted Bundy never had a dog, unless it was to abuse him.)

Talk about your two years in the Peace Corps. ("I was lucky. I got posted to Micronesia.") It's best to talk about what you learned from the natives, rather than how you helped them.

Talk about how you believe in tithing. When your prey asks if you do that, say, "I wouldn't suggest it for others if I didn't do it myself."

But there are other, more subtle ways to communicate that you're a Nice Guy.

One way is to pretend to be worried about another friend. Most people worry more about themselves than about anyone else; only a Nice Guy frets for others.

Get a sheepish look on your face whenever you're embarrassed. (Not so nice people are less prone to embarrassment.) If you're not sure you can convey this emotion with your expression, just cover your eyes with your hand and incline your head forward.

Assume the best intentions from everybody else. This may make you look a little naive, but will subtly communicate that you are motivated only by good intentions yourself.

SITUATION: You're telling an anecdote about your vacation in Estonia.

STIFF: "Anyway, this incredibly beautiful girl started gesturing to me in sign language that she wanted me to come home with her, and my buddies were all egging me on to do it ... but I didn't know what to do. I mean I wanted to, but I just felt so awkward. I guess I should have gone."

BOOR: "... so I went back to her room and fucked her. It was great, 'cause afterward I didn't have to talk to her at all."

CHARMER: "... but I didn't really see the point. I mean, we didn't even speak the same language—who knew if we really had anything in common?"

Be Discreet

Men and women like to be treated differently after a sexual liaison. Most men like to be thought of as studs, so unless he has some compelling reason why it needs to be kept quiet (i.e., he's married or he's your boss), a woman needn't worry too much about discretion.

If you're a man, you must zip it, period. Women like to hear gossip, but they also know that if you give away others' secrets, you'll give away theirs as well, so they will not confide in you—or go to bed with you.

So keep in mind that passing along common knowledge is excusable, and even a scoop you came by secondhand is forgivable, but betraying a firsthand confidence is not. And an affair with a woman is de facto firsthand.

SITUATION: Your prey asks you point-blank if you slept with a certain woman. (You did.)
STIFF: "Uh … ask her." (This is tacit admission.)
BOOR: "Oh yeah! She was really horny, too! I'm telling you, that bitch loved taking it up the ass."
CHARMER: (shaking head ruefully) "No, but what I wouldn't have given …"

Quelling Jealousy

When a rival experiences a triumph, even if it's not at our expense, we all feel a certain natural resentment. If you can extinguish that feeling in your prey, he will be grateful.

Let's say your prey's archrival Robert just received tenure at his university, something your prey doesn't have. Make it clear you're thinking along the same lines your prey is:

"Oh boy, he'll really be intolerable now."

"I can certainly think of guys who deserve it more."

"It could have happened to a nicer guy."

"Now people are going to hate him more than ever." (This should provoke a smile.)

Then tell your prey, "They've done studies of happiness that show that whatever triumphs or sorrows you experience, after three months you just return to the same emotional baseline you've been genetically programmed to be at. Nothing we accomplish really has any long-term effect on our happiness." (Don't tell your prey this if he's the one who just scored a big triumph.)

Add, for emphasis, "Robert will be the same miserable prick he always was." This will make your prey feel better.

Continue on, "I know Robert. He won't be able to enjoy it. It'll drive him crazy that other people are making more money than he is. Plus, he'll still be tortured by the thought that he's not at Harvard."

"And it certainly won't make up for the fact that he's so ugly and obnoxious." (Or whatever his weak points are.)

SITUATION: Your prey's worst enemy just won the lottery.

STIFF: "Wow ... what luck."

BOOR: "Ha! You must be eating your heart out!"

CHARMER: "You know, practically every lottery winner I ever heard of had his life go to pieces afterward. Everyone comes to them with their hands out, they become alcoholics, they get in trouble with the law, they don't factor in the taxes they owe, they eventually go broke. It's pretty much guaranteed."

The Massage

One of the best ways to ingratiate yourself is to make your prey feel good physically. Massage his shoulders, gently squeezing and lifting the trapezius muscle. People's shoulders are always tense, so this will feel good. It also feels good to have your scalp massaged (we're all like dogs that way), so if your prey is not too fussy about his hairdo, lightly scratch his head.

This technique works for both sexes, on both sexes, but you must take care not to make it seem sexual. The best way to do that is to just say, "I don't want you to think I'm coming on to you, because I'm not." If you want to, you can jokingly add, "Not that I don't *want* to, it's just that I know *you* wouldn't be interested." (Once again, this line works for both sexes, on both sexes, though you have to be careful if you're a woman giving one to a man, or if you're dealing with someone of the same sex who's severely homophobic.)

You needn't stop at the shoulders and scalp. You can do his neck (gently), or his upper back. (Venturing south of that *will* make it seem as if you're making a pass.)

Do this often enough and eventually your relationship should turn Pavlovian: your prey will just automatically relax when he's around you.

SITUATION: Your prey is sitting down and you walk up to him from behind.
STIFF: Says, "Hi John," forcing him to turn around to see who it is."
BOOR: Grabs him by the neck and squeezes painfully, saying, "Hey guy" in a gleeful tone of voice, happy to be hurting him.

CHARMER: Says, "You look like you've had a hard day," and proceeds to give him a massage.

Body Language

Entire books have been written about body language, and the nonverbal messages you send via your stance and facial expressions often speak louder—and more eloquently—than anything you say. So it's vital to have some awareness of what you're doing in that realm.

First, and most importantly, pay attention to your facial expression. It's best to have your eyes light up when you see your prey, and to break into a smile from time to time. But these are hard to fake and can easily turn into a forced smile or grimace. Even worse are the wince, the wrinkled nose, and any other look that communicates worry, consternation, or disgust.

If all else fails, just try to remain expressionless. If you feel tension overcoming your face, place the heel of both hands on your eyebrows and rub them sideways as if you're tired. This will effectively render you expressionless, at least temporarily. (This is not to be confused with placing one hand over your eyes in an "Oh no!" gesture.) And don't yawn if you can help it.

Drumming your fingers, twiddling your thumbs, and looking at your watch are gestures that indicate boredom. (In fact, these are often done on purpose, which makes them worse, in a way.)

Much has been made of "open" versus "closed" body positions, which are supposed to represent whether you are open to your prey or not. The message that you want to send is, of course, that you're open. So don't cross your arms while talking to him, or make "blocking" positions with your arms or legs.

Don't make a steeple with your ten fingertips, which is an expression of superiority.

Never looking into your prey's eyes means you don't like him. A nose-holding gesture whenever he talks means you are put off by what he has to say. Moving away from him, or even just pulling your head back, means the same thing.

Putting your hand over your mouth means you are guarded.

Biting your lower lip while baring your upper teeth indicates outright hostility. (Baring the fangs is a universal expression of hostility in the animal kingdom, of which we are a part.)

Leaning forward indicates enthusiasm.

Imitating your prey's posture generally means that you agree with him, and maybe even want to emulate him.

Putting an arm around someone's shoulders is a nominally friendly gesture, but be aware that it also expresses dominance.

Interestingly, staying perfectly still can have a disconcerting effect on the other person, although they are generally unaware of it.

SITUATION: Your prey tells you a story.

STIFF: Nods frequently to indicate he is listening, stands awkwardly, moves spasmodically from time to time, and keeps a fixed smile on his face that gradually turns into a grimace.

BOOR: Never once looks at him, yawns loudly, looks at his watch, shakes his head disgustedly, and makes a circular motion with his hand as if to say, "Hurry up!"

CHARMER: Faces his prey squarely and looks him in the eye. He leans forward as if he wants to hear every last word his prey says, the hint of amusement in his face slowly turning into outright delight.

PART III
Self-Deprecation

Self-deprecation is the essence of charm. If you can hold your own worst faults up to the light and laugh at them, it means you're not likely to get angry at any comment your prey makes. A reliable rule of thumb is that the more people lie to themselves, the more often they get "offended" whenever people say something that reflects negatively on their self-image. In psychology, such people are known as narcissistic personalities. You want to show, through skillful self-deprecation, that you are a completely un-narcissistic personality.

While reading the following chapters, please keep in mind that you cannot say things that are obviously untrue, otherwise you will appear falsely modest—the kiss of death for any would-be charmer. A handsome guy who complains about his ugliness merely comes across phony, or as if he's fishing for compliments. You must instead have the courage to pick apart your weak points. If you are a harsh enough self-critic, you will even take away others' desire to criticize you. Being self-deprecating actually renders you invulnerable, in a way: once you have publicly probed your own sore spots, no one else's insults will carry quite the same sting. If you can make a joke out of those sore spots, your invulnerability will be apparent to others.

Your Looks

Nothing is more central to your self-image than your face. If you can make fun of yours, you'll come across much more simpatico.

Shrug, "I'd like to think of myself as good-looking; the problem is, I own a mirror."

Next time you're in front of a mirror, say, "Mirror, mirror, on the wall, who is the ugliest of them all?" Then put your ear to the mirror and say, "Me? Well, can't say I'm surprised."

Suggest, "You could put my picture on your front door, scare away the robbers."

If your prey ever sees a picture of you as a child and comments on your cuteness, explain, "I'm sort of the ugly duckling story in reverse—I grew up to be an ugly duck."

If there are four of you sitting at a table, say, "Hey, I'm the fourth best-looking guy here!"

If your prey ever says, "I'm having a bad hair day," reply, "Don't feel bad, I'm having a bad hair life."

If you have a good-looking body and an ordinary face, say, "My problem is, from the neck up I look like Quasimodo."

Point out your resemblance to an uglier version of yourself. If you think you look like Brad Pitt, point out your resemblance to Philip Seymour Hoffman. If you think you look like Winona Ryder, point out your resemblance to Roseanne Barr. If you think you look like the young Marlon Brando, point out your resemblance to the old Marlon Brando. And so on.

If you're truly ugly, say, "Sometimes, I look in the mirror and can't believe how handsome I am. I've had offers from all the top modeling agencies. My biggest problem is that people are so blinded by my beauty, they don't see the real me inside."

In case your prey doesn't realize you're joking, add, "Actually, I'm like Medusa. Look at me too long, and you turn to stone."

SITUATION: The subject of your appearance comes up.
STIFF: "I'm okay, I guess."
BOOR: "I'm a damn good-looking guy. Everybody says I look like George Clooney."
CHARMER: "I'm thinking about going to a plastic surgeon, have him change every single feature on my face. No one would recognize me, but at least that way I'd get a fresh start."

Your Intelligence

It's a truism that dumb people say they're smart, and smart people say they're dumb. So if you want to appear smart, play down your intelligence. (By the way, you *are* smart if you're reading this book.)

If your prey ever compliments you on your intelligence, reply, "How smart can I be?" Then cite some dumb thing you've done.

If he knows about your eight hundred math SAT, pooh-pooh it. Say, "You know how some people say that they're actually smart, it's just that they don't test well? I'm just the opposite. I'm actually dumb, I just test really well."

Or say, "I'm still trying to figure out how that happened. You know how the SATs are mostly multiple choice? I actually guessed on about half the questions. I was just incredibly lucky." Your prey won't believe you, but at least he won't think you're conceited.

If your prey compliments you on your academic accomplishments, say, "Thanks. I'm actually fairly dumb, I just study hard." Intelligence is intimidating, bookwormishness is not.

Or respond, "Know what the definition of an intellectual is? Someone who thinks he's smart."

If your prey compliments you on your eloquence, reply, "Better glib than smart. I never really know what I'm talking about, but I do sound good, don't I?"

If your prey compliments you on your memory after you remember a phone number or something similar, reply, "I'm sort of like Rain Man—with, unfortunately, the same set of social skills."

If you've achieved some type of real world success that proves your brilliance beyond the shadow of a doubt (e.g., you have a Ph.D. in physics), say, "I'm no smarter than anyone else. I just happen to be interested in that subject. Can you imagine someone so boring he actually finds physics interesting?"

The idea is not to leave your prey thinking that you're actually stupid, just that you're not stuck-up.

If you are in fact of average intelligence—or less—emphasize your lack of intellectual accomplishment. Say you dropped out of high school (even if you didn't). Cite your low SATs. A lot of people are ashamed of such things, as if they're some deep, dark secret that should never see the light of day. Do the opposite. Turn your "stupidity" into a joke, and it will lose its power over you.

Say, "Sometimes, when I walk, I have to remind myself, left foot, right foot, left foot … Stuff that you take for granted doesn't come so easy to me."

SITUATION: Your prey asks how you did on your SATs. (You got a thousand, combined.)
STIFF: "I don't remember" (even though he actually does).
BOOR: "Fourteen hundred and ten" (rounding up by four hundred).
CHARMER: (brightly) "I got an eight hundred. That was math and verbal combined."

If You're Fat

One of the first things people judge us by is our weight. Even though all the available evidence indicates we are born with a certain number of fat cells and there's little we can do about it, there remains a sense of moral disapproval about obesity. If you're fat, you can disperse some of this by joking about it.

Say, "I'm a Rubenesque beauty. In the South Pacific, I'd be considered a real catch."

"I'm not just some scrawny little two-hundred-and-fifty-pounder."

If someone asks your weight, answer, "Three thirty—hey, it's not like I weigh three forty or anything."

"Don't laugh. If we were ever on a desert island, I'd be the last to starve. I've actually been preparing for that eventuality all my life. *And* I have the most protection from the cold."

If the subject turns to athletics, say, "A lot of people have told me I'd be good at sumo."

If you're ever dispirited, sigh, "And I'm not even jolly."

If you do something singular, and somebody comments on it, reply, "There's only one Nick Casanova—although, from a distance, it does look as though there are two."

Joking about your fat won't make it disappear, but it will make it weigh a little less heavy.

SITUATION: Your prey asks how much you weigh. (You weigh two thirty, much of it fat.)
STIFF: (sighs) "Two twenty-six. I've got to get back on my diet."
BOOR: "Fuck you!"
CHARMER: "Two thirty. I'm proud to report, I've won my battle against anorexia."

If You're Skinny

Although America is a nation of dieters, people who are too skinny are also self-conscious. But skinniness represents another opportunity to be self-deprecating, particularly if someone else brings the subject up.

"People occasionally tell me that I'm lucky to be skinny; they're crazy. I want to be muscular. I'm like one of those skeletons people hang on their porch at Halloween."

"It's a little embarrassing in a storm 'cause sometimes I just get blown away."

"Despite appearances, I am not anorexic. Because anorexic people don't realize they're thin, whereas I do, and I hate it."

"I'm like the before picture in those old Charles Atlas ads. And it's true, people do kick sand in my face."

"I honestly think that at a very basic level, people don't take me seriously because I don't represent any sort of physical threat to them."

"I'd like to say I'm fashionably thin, but really, scrawny is so much more apt."

"If you took me and Chris Farley, and averaged us out, you'd have someone who looked just about right."

"I stay away from romance because of a poem I once heard: Fat and Skinny went to bed, Fat rolled over and Skinny was dead."

SITUATION: You're a guy who's six feet tall and weighs 137 pounds. Someone compliments you for being thin.
STIFF: "Oh ... thanks, I guess."
BOOR: "I couldn't stand to be a fatso like you."

CHARMER: "I'll probably be one of those guys who in middle age just transitions directly from being skinny to being paunchy, without ever being a happy medium."

If You're Short

Being short is generally considered a social disadvantage, but if you joke about it, you can make it seem less so.

If you ever boast, explain, "It's my inferiority complex. Comes with being five foot six."

Add, "I'm five foot six, but my ego is around seven foot six."

"I've tried those lifts you wear in your shoes, but they don't seem to make much difference."

If someone compliments you on, say, your ability at badminton, reply, "I'm a miniature badminton champion."

"If I were a dog, I'd be a Chihuahua."

Say, "It's a little known fact, but Attila the Hun was actually a dwarf." (This is true.) Then add, "So were George Washington and Abraham Lincoln. And Michael Jordan." Claiming these famously tall people as kin will be interpreted as self-deprecation.

SITUATION: Your prey asks how tall you are. (You're five foot six.)
STIFF: "Five feet six inches."
BOOR: "Five eight, what's it to you?"
CHARMER: "Five six. I think it's why I have even more of a Napoleonic complex that Bonaparte himself actually had."

Your Job

In America, for better or worse, you pretty much are your job. So if you have a higher status occupation than your prey, to make him feel better, disparage your job.

Start by quoting a salary that's less than what he makes. If that's not believable, quote one that is only slightly more. When he says he thought corporate lawyers made more, reply, "That's when you move up in the organization. I'm a very small cog in a very big machine. I think I'm the lowest paid guy in my department."

When he asks you how you can afford such nice things, reply, "Credit. Problem is, I'm maxed out on all my cards at the moment. I'll be in hock for the next twenty years. I feel as if I'm on one of those never-ending treadmills that I'll never get off. It's like a nightmare, except I'm awake."

"The nature of what I do is the same day in and day out. My eyes glaze, I see double, but I keep slogging away. The standard boilerplate I spew out I could do in my sleep. I swear, a monkey could do what I do. And probably do it better, since it wouldn't get bored. It's really not that different than being on an assembly line."

One line sure to quell jealousy is, "I have a boss who is the most belligerent, self-righteous hypocrite you've ever met. And he seems to enjoy humiliating me in front of other people."

"When you work with a guy who takes all the credit and none of the blame, you get left with none of the credit and all of the blame. Unfortunately, I need my job."

Even if you're the star rainmaker at an investment bank, tell your prey, "My job is basically to kiss ass. If my boss makes some incredibly lame joke, I have to laugh like it's the funniest thing I ever heard."

"My official job title is Vice President, but my unofficial job description is 'toady.' If the boss wants coffee, I get it. I'm basically a gofer."

"I'm sorta the combination butt-boy and scapegoat of my office. These bankers are the most sociopathic people you'll ever meet. If they weren't doing that, they'd be serial killers. As it is, they're all serial character assassins."

No matter what your job, you can make it sound horrible.

SITUATION: You're an investment banker with a promising career at one of the top Wall Street firms. Your prey says enviously that you must be making a ton of money.
STIFF: "I don't know ... I guess."
BOOR: (gleefully) "I could probably buy and sell you ten times over."
CHARMER: "On an hourly basis, I think junior bankers like me barely make minimum wage—the hours are horrendous. See these wrinkles? This job is taking years off my life."

Summarize Your Occupation

When first meeting someone, it can be very helpful, after they ask what you do, to have a line that encapsulates the public perception of your occupation in a disparaging way.

"I'm a lawyer—when I'm not chasing ambulances, I'm mounting frivolous lawsuits that waste valuable court time."

"I'm a teacher—one of those people responsible for our declining SATs."

"I'm in advertising—I make a living trying to convince people to buy things they don't need."

"I'm a doctor—my specialties are urology and Medicaid rip-off."

"I'm a cop—it's a great job if you enjoy planting evidence and roughing up innocent bystanders."

"I'm a reporter—when I'm not shoving cameras in grieving relatives' faces, I'm raking muck."

"I'm an automotive engineer—one of those guys helping get rid of the ozone layer."

"I'm an insurance executive—you know, a glorified pencil pusher." (The "pencil pusher" description can be applied to virtually any white-collar job.)

"I work construction—I'm one of those obnoxious guys in the hard hats who whistles at the girls as they walk by."

You can actually use such statements as a springboard to do a little boasting about what you do. ("Seriously, what I actually do is …")

As long as you're aware of what the popular image of your field is, virtually any job can be excused. ("I'm an interrogation officer. You know how they have the good cop/bad cop routine? Well I'm the bad cop. It's my job to make Abu Ghraib look like a country club.")

SITUATION: A girl at a party asks what you do for a living.

STIFF: "I'm a stockbroker."

BOOR: "I'm a personal financial consultant at Merrill. Number one producer in my office for the last three years, actually. It's how I afford the condo in Florida."

CHARMER: "I'm a stockbroker—you know, one of those people who gets rich selling Enron and WorldCom to widows."

Your Athletic Ability

When asked about your sport, you must do the opposite of what your instincts compel you to: you must put your athletic career down in a way your prey will find reassuring, especially if he was a mediocre athlete himself. Whatever your sport was, you can find some way to put it—and more importantly, yourself—down.

If your prey was a nonathlete, start by commenting on the silliness of athletics: "I was on the football team. People take that sport so seriously, the coaches especially. You'd think they were generals in World War II. And they try to imbue the sport with moral qualities that have nothing to do with it." Nonathletes often regard athletics the way most people regard hopscotch, as a time-wasting diversion, so your prey will agree.

Continue, "Football is the dumbest sport in the world. We're human beings, not rams. I was lucky not to be permanently injured, unlike a lot of my teammates who are still gimping around. Of course, that's 'cause I was third string and never got to play."

No matter what your sport, there is a way to put yourself down:

"I did cross country, as you can tell from my build."

"I was a gymnast. It was either that or be a jockey."

"I was a baseball player. That's why I have such a great cardiovascular system."

"I wasn't tall enough for basketball, strong enough for football, or tough enough for cross country, so I went out for the chess team."

"I was a miler, but it wasn't until senior year that I could actually run the entire mile without stopping. They timed the other guys with a stopwatch, but with me they just used a sundial."

"My wrestling coach called me 'the turtle' because once I was on my back I was helpless."

If you played a team sport, and are asked what position you played, reply, "Mostly I played bench warmer. My goal was to make second string, which I never quite did."

Add, "I was one of those guys who made the other guys look good. Can't have stars if there aren't scrubs, right?"

"I scored three goals one game, but two of them were in our own goal. The coaches used to get so mad at me, just 'cause I had a little problem with dyslexia."

Or just put down your own toughness: "I wanted to be a running back, but I was always scared of getting hit. When I finally got put in a game, there was this really big guy on the other team coming at me, so I just threw the ball away. I'd rather have the coach mad at me than have had that monster crush me."

Say, "My basic problem is that I'm just not strong enough. I've considered taking steroids, but they put acne on your back, give you kidney and liver damage, make you more prone to cancer and heart attacks, give you steroid rages, and shrink your testicles…. I'd still take them, but the problem is my testicles are too small to start with."

SITUATION: Your prey asks if you played a sport in school.
STIFF: "I swam."
BOOR: "I was state champ in the hundred fly."
CHARMER: "I swam. My coach would always give the other guys time goals. With me, he'd be happy if I didn't drown." Shrugs, "They always alerted the lifeguards when my event came up."

Your House

Burt Reynolds, back when he was still considered a macho icon (in the 1970s), was once interviewed by Barbara Walters in his home. When she entered, he said, "Looks like a bullfighter threw up in here, doesn't it?" The seemingly offhand comment, tossed off casually, was perfect: it captured his macho image and simultaneously made fun of it. You should find a way to make fun of your own house the same way.

If you have a big house, the idea is to make your prey feel the least jealousy possible when he sees it.

After he oohs and aahs about your mansion, say, "This thing is a white elephant. I've done nothing but pour money into it, and it's always hungry for more." Even if you paid for your house out of your spare change, confide, "I'm going to be working forever just to pay it off."

When you get to the master bedroom, say, "These are the servants' quarters." Shrug, "I'm the servant around here, so …"

If any of the rooms are not well lit, explain, "I'm partial to the mausoleum look … I also like subways as a motif."

If your lawn is not well tended, say, "You know how they name big estates? I call this place 'Weed Gardens.' It was either that or 'Termite City.'"

Make disparaging remarks about the furniture. "I opted to decorate in neo-dormitory. It's hard to match styles when you buy everything at garage sales."

If your house is small, say, "No one would ever guess I'm a billionaire from my house; I like to keep my secret under wraps." Point at a bare wall and say, "When I get my Picasso, that's where I intend to hang it."

If there are any broken windows, say, "I wanted a well ventilated house. Fresh air is important to me."

"When I bought this property, the house was considered a tear-down. Still is, actually."

"This is what you call an unpretentious house. If it were any more unpretentious, I guess it would have to be a corrugated tin roof shanty."

Gesture at your rec room and say, "We hold our formal balls in here. I wanted a house that just screamed 'high society.'"

If you live in a studio apartment, explain, "I actually own this entire apartment building. I just chose to live in this apartment."

Point at the four sides of the room and say, "That's the East Wing, this is the West Wing, that's the North Wing, and that's the South Wing." Then walk a couple steps over to the other side of he room. When your prey next speaks, cup your hand around your ear and say, "Sorry, can't hear you, I'm all the way over in the North Wing."

SITUATION: Your prey compliments you on your spacious house.
STIFF: "I guess it is pretty big."
BOOR: "I couldn't live like a peon anymore." (Despite the fact that his prey lives in a small house.)
CHARMER: "This house is as much work as having a child, but without the emotional reward. If I had to do it over again, I'd buy a smaller house."

Your Car

Self-deprecating comments about your car fall into the same two basic categories that comments about your house do, depending on whether it's fancy or not.

If it's a fancy car, you have to make fun of yourself for having bought it. Say, "The World Trade Center bombing [substitute any recent disaster] really made me re-examine my values, think long and hard about what really mattered to me: family, friends, and so on. Anyway, after some extensive soul-searching … I went out and bought a Lexus."

Tap the roof of the car and say, "I had to dip into my children's educational fund in order to finance it, but you gotta admit, it looks good on me."

"After driving this thing around for a month, I had an epiphany: I am the human equivalent of a Lexus LS430. I guess that's why people buy cars like this, because they see themselves that way."

Or reflect, "Before I got this car, I used to look down on people who put too much stock in their cars." Shrug, "These days I just look down on people who don't have as nice a car."

If your prey actually seems jealous of your car, show buyer's remorse: "You know, I actually feel sort of stupid having bought this. It was fun for about a month, now it's just another gas guzzler."

If, on the other hand, you drive a cheap car, say, "This is how I proclaim my status to the world." Raise your arms above your head and cry out, "I *have arrived!*"

Say, "It was either this or a Rolls."

"This is the kind of car that the valets at fancy restaurants always like to park out front."

Tap the hood and say, "Four hundred horses." Then shrug, "Actually, getting a muscle car would have been wasted on me. I drive like an old lady anyway."

"You know, a lot of people are under the misimpression that that car James Bond drove in *Goldfinger* was an Aston Martin. It wasn't. It was a Corolla." Nod as if you're positive about this.

SITUATION: Your prey compliments you on your Lexus LS430.
BOOR: "This is some set of wheels, eh?"
STIFF: "Oh, thanks."
CHARMER: "I wanted the kind of car that proclaimed Mid-Life Crisis very loudly." Add, "Actually, this is how I make up for being short and fat."

Your Clothes

It's always better to look like a guy who knows fashion but just doesn't care than a yokel who doesn't understand it in the first place.

If you're dressed like a slob, say, "I'm striving for crack-addict chic," or "I'm trying to bring grunge back."

"Actually, I'm about to change the oil in my car."

"I don't think I'm too old to still be dressing like a student. Some people still go to school at forty-five, you know. For all you know, I'm taking extension courses."

If your shirt has holes in it, shrug, "Ninety-nine percent of the shirt is still here. It's only the 1 percent that's missing."

"Just call me Beau Brummel. I've always been a bit of a dandy."

If your pants are short, say, "Well you never know when those pipes in the basement are going to burst," or, "I just got back from clam digging."

If your colors are wrong, say, "I'm color blind. Just consider yourself lucky I'm not wearing plaids and stripes."

If you're dressed in a lumberjack shirt and jeans in a situation where everybody else is dressier, say, "Sorry, I was just chopping down some trees and didn't have time to change."

If you've been wearing the same clothes for several days, and your prey calls attention to that, reply, "Hey, for me, that's just getting warmed up."

An all-purpose defense is, "I figure I'm doing well if I get the right shirt button in the right hole."

Or just explain, "I lost a bet."

Or, "To be honest, I'm a cross-dresser. I don't know that much about men's clothes, but you should see me when I'm dressed up as a woman—I'm the height of fashion."

On the rare occasion that you dress up, if somebody comments on it, say, "I look like a mobster all dressed up to go to church."

Or, "I figure if I have nice clothes, people will overlook my personality."

Or, "I honestly feel like a little kid dressed up in his father's clothes."

SITUATION: Your prey criticizes your somewhat dingy clothes.
STIFF: "These aren't so bad."
BOOR: "You're not exactly what I'd call a fashion plate either."
CHARMER: "You're right, I guess it's time for another trip to Goodwill. Not to get rid of these, but to pick up a new outfit."

"Men Are Such Pigs"

In the war between the sexes, each side has its standard complaints: men, especially married men, like to talk about how illogical and overly emotional women are; women complain about how insensitive and selfish men are. If you are a man trying to score points with a woman, you can make great strides by sympathizing with the women's viewpoint.

Start by saying, "You know, I hate to say it, but the world really would be a better place if it were run by women."

Continue, "Men have these huge egos that make them do battle over the silliest things. They all have this tremendous need to prove their masculinity, and it really makes them sort of pathetic."

"So many guys are just gross. There's no other way to put it. And most of them will have sex with anything that moves. They're like barnyard animals."

Lest your prey think you're gay, say, "I swear, I'm a fag at heart." (A gay man wouldn't put it that way.) Add confidentially, "I even like going shopping for clothes. I'm a woman in the body of a man."

Even if your idea of perfect bliss is an afternoon of watching football with the guys, say, "So many guys just love to watch sports on TV. It would be one thing if they participated, but they just sit there and watch. It's *so* boring."

These statements should make you look a bit less porcine, no matter what a swine you really are.

All these comments work best if you're naturally macho. If your prey thinks you a bit wimpy to start with, this chapter is not for you.

SITUATION: You're a man talking to a woman, and the subject of sex differences arises.

STIFF: "Yeah, I guess there are differences."

BOOR: "Women are such a pain. Once a month, like clockwork, it never fails. Of course, some women act like they're on the rag thirty days a month."

CHARMER: "To tell the truth, I get along better with my female friends than with my male friends. I just enjoy their company more, feel we have more in common."

"Women Are Such Twits"

If you're a woman dealing with men, the path to instant ingratiation is to tell your prospect how emotional and illogical most women are. Even if you don't believe it—or if you are this way yourself—you will score points by asserting this. In fact, your prospect will probably not be able to believe his luck in stumbling across a woman with a male viewpoint (every man's ideal woman).

Get right to the point: "I feel sorry for guys. Most girls are such idiots. And the stuff they care about—shopping and clothes—yecch! I'd really rather just hang out and watch football."

Continue: "I hate the way those strident feminists—and what wonderful senses of humor *they* have—talk about equal pay for equal work, then they want the qualifications changed for the firemen's test so that women don't have to meet the same standards. And most of them still expect the guy to pay when they go out on a date."

Add, "So many women just want to see how much money they can get a guy to spend on them. It's disgusting."

"I think it's hard being a guy. You're the one who has to ask the girl out on a date, and suffer the rejection if she doesn't want to go."

"And even when it comes to sex—a woman can just lie there, and a guy will be satisfied, but you guys have to perform and risk that embarrassment. It must be so nerve-wracking."

If you're not beautiful to start with, this kind of talk can turn you from a five into an eight.

SITUATION: You're a woman talking to a man, and the subject of sex differences arises.

STIFF: "I don't think that there are that many innate differences, it's just that we're raised differently."

BOOR: "Men always think they're so great. I *hate* them."

CHARMER: "I don't know how you put up with our mood swings. I really don't."

"I'm Nothing Special—Just Your Average Joe"

Most of us are not nearly so unique as we imagine ourselves. In fact, the rare person is the one who recognizes just how average he is. So, to demonstrate to your prey that you're a cut above the rest, claim the opposite.

Say, "I wish I could say I was something special, but the sad truth is, I'm really not. I'm just an average guy, with typically slobbish tastes—I like girls, beer, and cars, not necessarily in that order."

Remember, the key is to say you're "average," not "normal." If you claim normalcy, a slightly different concept, your prey will wonder what abnormality you're trying to hide: a deviant sexuality, a sociopathic personality, or a drug habit? The word "average," on the other hand, merely implies a lack of distinction.

Say, "I'd *like* to be a star of some sort, but it seems my destiny to be an also-ran."

This routine is more effective if you actually are a star of some sort, be it in sports, academics, business, or any other field. (If you are in fact good at nothing, you may not want to use this routine.) If you are a star, your prey will probably point this out, which will offer yet another opportunity for "modesty."

You don't want to give concrete evidence of your ordinariness, lest your prey think you really are just an ordinary schmo. So keep most of your comments aimed at your character (this shows more insight anyway):

"Sometimes I think I have too much pride. And I'm susceptible to flattery. Egos can be pretty silly things." Everyone is guilty of this.

"Emotionally I'm the same as everyone else. I'm up, I'm down, I seem to have very little control over what mood I'm in." (Who does?)

"I'm slow to anger, but when I get really angry, I can feel like killing someone." (Who can't?)

If you really want to show perspective, place yourself in class and time: "I'm a typical middle-class kid born in America in the 1970s. I know my culture, but very little outside it. I'm familiar with MTV and the Internet. But I can't fix a car, do plumbing, or carpentry. Put me in the jungle and I'd be dead in minutes."

SITUATION: You're on a first date with your prey, who tells you you're quite special.
STIFF: (shrugging) "Oh, I don't know."
BOOR: Nods and looks pleased that she recognizes his status.
CHARMER: "I'm a nobody. Always have been, always will be." (With this as a lead in, a small boast is now palatable.) "But I can be lots of fun."

"I'm Inexperienced with Girls"

An obnoxious man boasts about his sexual conquests. (He thinks he will inspire admiration, but more often inspires resentment and/or skepticism.) The charmer lies the other way.

Both men and women find this reassuring. Men like to hear this because it makes them feel worldly by comparison. Women like to hear it because it means you're not a womanizer, so she's not just another potential notch on the bedpost.

Tell your male friend, "You've obviously had a lot of conquests, but my life has been rather dull in that regard." To inject a note of realism, you might add, "Not that I haven't thought about it a lot."

If you're with a woman, and she asks why you have a reputation as a rake, profess mystification. (Wolves dress in sheep's clothing for a reason.) Even if your mystification is met with disbelief, at least this will make you seem modest.

At some point, say, "I'm just not very good with girls. I guess I just don't have the seduction gene."

Add, "Most of the time, I don't even have the nerve to make a move on them." (Everyone except an out and out sociopath loses his nerve occasionally; this will just make you seem normal.)

If your prey is a woman, don't continue in this vein too long lest she think you a complete dud. So add, "All I've ever had in my entire life is three long-term girlfriends." This indicates that your problem is seduction, not sex, since presumably no girl would stay with a guy who didn't satisfy her. It also implies you have no problem with commitment—a big plus for most women.

If you're an attractive woman talking to a less attractive female, use a similar tactic. Just say you never get asked out by guys. One occasionally hears beautiful women complain about this; it's usually not credible, but it's still reassuring for your prey to hear. Misery loves company, or, in this case, loves to hear that you don't have company.

SITUATION: Your prey asks you how many women you've slept with.
STIFF: "I don't like to talk about that."
BOOR: "Forty" (even though it's really four).
CHARMER: "Four" (even though it's really forty).

Be Racist against Yourself

We must all take care to tiptoe very gently around the minefield of excessive honesty when it comes to America's great taboo: race. But one of the best ways to put your prey off his guard is to be self-deprecating about your own group. Merely point out a few of the pejorative stereotypes about your own ethnicity, and use them as an explanation for your lapses. Your prey will immediately warm up to you as he finds out that you don't take these stereotypes—or yourself—too seriously.

There's a self-deprecatory comment for every ethnicity:

Let's say you're of Japanese descent and you're using your camera. Shrug, "I can't help it. I'm Japanese, I just have to snap away."

If you're Italian and you suffer a lapse in personal hygiene, say, "What do you expect, I'm Italian. After we wake up in the morning, we use the bed sheets for tablecloths."

If you make a dumb mistake, shrug, "I'm Polish. You've heard all the jokes."

If you hurt someone by accident, say, "Sorry, I'm Serbian. We like to hurt people."

"I'm Latin. We're demonstrative."

"I'm Swiss. No sense of humor."

"I'm Armenian. Lying is second nature to us."

"I'm German. We've been bred to follow orders."

"I'm British. We don't approve of sex."

These comments needn't just be about your ethnicity, they can be about your Americanism when you're abroad: "I'm an American. You know, big houses and big cars. And we love to bomb other countries whenever we get the chance. Oh, and I love McDonalds, too."

Most of the above "explanations" and ethnicities can be switched around as needed. This book would prefer not to open up the Pandora's Box of really invidious stereotypes, but you know what they are and which ones apply to your group. If you get the chance, use them against yourself.

SITUATION: Your hometown is Ottawa and you've just finished telling your Minnesotan friend a rather dull story.

STIFF: "Anyway, that's the end, I guess."

BOOR: Says, "Agh," and waves a dismissive hand at the Minnesotan, as if he's too dumb to understand the point of the story.

CHARMER: "You know, by *Canadian* standards, that was a really exciting story."

Make Fun of Your Own Wimpiness

All men are faced with a basic dilemma in life: to be macho, or not to be. If you choose the macho route, you must constantly prove yourself. You can't back down from fights, you can't shy away from dangerous sports, and you must toss down liquor like water.

Obviously, being a wimp is the wise, if ignominious, choice. But there is a way to ease the sting of your wimpiness, and that is to turn it into a joke.

At every opportunity, put yourself down:

"I met a guy the other day who was a Navy Seal. Boy was that emasculating. You have any idea what those guys have to do to become Seals? As just one part of their training, they do a parachute jump from such high altitude that they have to wear oxygen masks, and they have to do it in the middle of the night, and they do it into the ocean. You couldn't pay me enough to jump out of an airplane. I'm scared of the ocean—I don't even like to swim in a lake when I can't see the bottom. And to be honest, I'm sort of scared of the dark. I guess I'm not Seal material."

By exposing your cowardice to the light of day and laughing about it, you've turned it into something funny rather than a shameful secret. Conclude, "Thank God there are people like that to defend our country. If the Army were composed of people like me, we'd have been conquered a long time ago—by Guatemala."

Talk about the time you got beaten up by a girl. "At first I thought it was a joke, but then she started really whacking me, so I figured I had to respond in kind. So I was getting ready to really haul off, when the next thing I knew she had me in an armlock and I was on the ground. I guess she knew ju jitsu or something." Shake your head, "That's cheating as far as I'm concerned. The bitch." (Women will love this story.)

"One time a dog treed me, and I couldn't come down for over an hour. It was a Chihuahua, but you never know, it could have been rabid or something."

"I'm very easy to intimidate. Pretty much all you really have to do is say hi."

If you have a friend who's much larger and stronger than you, threaten to beat him up in front of other people. (The emphasis in the previous sentence is on the word "friend"—you must choose someone good-natured who will play along with your little skit.) Bump chests with him. If you have to look straight up to stare him down, all the better. Snarl, "You even dream of disrespecting me and I'll rip your head off and piss down your neck! I swear to God I'll put my foot so far up your ass you'll be tasting shoe leather for the next two weeks." Then give him a shove for good measure. The sight of a toy poodle threatening a Rottweiler usually strikes people as funny.

SITUATION: Your prey sees a hairy, fat-bodied spider on her wall, and, terrified, asks you to get it for her.

STIFF: Reluctantly gathers a wad of tissue paper, and hesitantly dabs at it, but it darts off and disappears behind the sofa.

BOOR: Takes off his shoe and splats the spider against the wall, wipes his shoe on the sofa, then gestures at the wall and says, "You clean it up."

CHARMER: Says, "I'm scared of spiders, too. I usually get my daughter to squash them for me." Then swats the spider with his shoe and cleans off both his shoe and the wall with a piece of wet tissue paper.

If You Have a Reputation for Being Macho

If you want to make yourself truly invulnerable, the best way is to mock yourself. This way, if your nerve ever fails you, it won't be as if you failed to live up to some tough guy image.

If you ever find yourself boasting, add, "I guess real tough guys don't have to advertise the fact." Shrug, "I do."

If you've been lauded for some feat of strength, reply, "What I do for fun is run around and uproot oak trees."

Flex and ask, "Wanna feel my muscle?"

Musclemen often wear clothes that accentuate their musculature. If you're guilty of this, shrug, "I don't have much money—I can't afford shirts with sleeves." Strike an exaggerated bodybuilder pose.

"I have this need to see myself as the hero in a Schwarzenegger movie. The ironic thing is, I'm actually more the bully type." (No real bully ever refers to himself as such.) "If anyone fights back, I just fold."

Say, "My role model is Bluto. You know, the big guy in Popeye who was always trying to kidnap Olive Oyl. Ah, who am I kidding, my role model was Don Knotts."

Pretend to beat up your prey, throwing some mock punches at him and wrestling him (gently) to the ground.

If you ever actually do act tough in some situation, say, "I always go after it like I have something to prove, don't I? Who knows, maybe I do." Add, "My real problem is, whenever I try to act tough, I end up coming across like one of the Village People."

SITUATION: Your prey asks you about a fight you won.
STIFF: "Well … I did win."
BOOR: "I rearranged that asshole's face permanent."
CHARMER: "The argument did get pretty heated. I got my revenge though—I left without saying good-bye."

Taking a Compliment

The old fallback, "Thank you," works well enough under most circumstances. Fallback number two, "It's nice of you to say that," works even better.

It is also true that a little dose of self-deprecation goes a long way towards making you appear grounded:

"Thank you, but you go way too far."

"You're alone in that opinion, but that makes it all the more appreciated."

"That was exactly what my tattered psyche needed."

If you agree with the compliment but want to come across as if you don't, say, "You mock me."

"If I keep listening to you, I'm going to become really intolerable, so you better stop right now. I can feel my head getting bigger already."

"Thank you very much, but I'm an absolute novice compared to people who really know what they're doing."

You can always deflect a compliment back: "Wow, coming from the master himself, that's a real compliment."

If you're complimented on one of your possessions, reply, "That's how I affirm myself, through my possessions. I'm a very materialistic person."

Or just say, "It's how I make up for being ugly." (Or "stupid," or whatever suits you.)

SITUATION: Your prey compliments you on your new jacket.
STIFF: "Thanks."
BOOR: "Looks pretty good on me, don't it?"
CHARMER: "I've got the outer part nailed, it's the inner part that's a work in progress."

If He Looks at Your Photo Album

If your prey should by chance happen upon your photo album and leaf through it, it's best to have some self-deprecating comments on hand while you serve as tour guide.

You probably have some photos of yourself next to famous landmarks. Mock yourself for these. "This is the picture that proves I was actually at the Grand Canyon—as if anyone would care."

You may have had your picture taken with a famous person. Say, "That was the day Jimmy Carter got to have his picture taken with me. I'm sure he's got his copy of this photo in a prominent place in his house."

The easiest way to make fun of yourself is to mock the way you look in various shots. If you're the type who puts on a certain expression when posing, say, "That's my game face, as you can tell."

If a photo makes you look fat, say, "I'm thinking about putting this photo on my refrigerator door."

If your smile is obviously forced, point that out: "My smiles are always genuine."

If your prey sees a picture of you with your family, say, "Here we are, the Munsters."

If there are any shots of you in your bathing suit, say, "Here I am, showing off my lack of muscle tone."

If you have any shots of you standing next to your new car, say, "Here I am doing the original thing, posing with my car."

If you have a picture with an ex-girlfriend or ex-wife, say, "This is Sally and me, before she got sick of me."

SITUATION: Your prey sees a picture of your family and says how good-looking they are.
STIFF: "Thank you."
BOOR: "Good looks run in the genes I guess."
CHARMER: "It's so rare that all of us are out of jail at the same time, we thought we'd have our picture taken. Usually we're just a collection of mug shots."

"I May Be Fat, But At Least I'm Slow"

One of the most effective ways to put yourself down is to make a comment about yourself that starts off sounding as if it's going to turn into a boast, but turns out to be entirely self-demeaning:

"Hey—watch your step. I may be skinny, but I'm weak."

"I may be a little slow on the uptake, but I'm dumb."

"I'm aggressive, but obnoxious."

"I'm short, but Napoleonic."

"I'm shy, but easily cowed."

"I may be a little selfish, but on the other hand, I'm very greedy."

"I'm long-winded, but boring."

"I'm thrifty, but cheap."

"I may not be the best masseur in the world, but I'm also a lousy lover."

"A lot of the time I'm pretty dull, but sometimes I'm *really* dull."

If modesty is good, these lines are doubly good. This type of joke will render you funny but charming.

SITUATION: You've just blurted out to your prey, a dancer, that she didn't look that good in her rehearsal.
STIFF: "But ... well, it did seem like you were trying really hard."
BOOR: "You need to practice more, or something."
CHARMER: "I may be blunt, but on the other hand, I'm undiplomatic."

"I Have No Self-Discipline"

Even if you're Mr. Willpower, whose friends all marvel at your determination, your prey will find it reassuring to hear that you have no self-discipline, especially if he has little himself.

"Two years ago, my New Year's resolution was no more drinking. Last year's resolution was more realistic: no more than one drink a day, three times a week. But I couldn't even do that. This year, my resolution is to only get drunk every other night. To be honest, that's fallen by the wayside, too. But one thing I can still be proud of: I never, ever start drinking before ten thirty in the morning."

"That darn refrigerator keeps calling to me, 'I'm full of goodies, come see, come see….' I tried keeping it empty, but that ended up getting too expensive because I would just order out every night. I tried putting a padlock on it, but that only slowed me down a little. I'd get my stomach stapled, but the thought of the operation scares me too much. My idea of fun is to look through a Harry and David catalogue, but that's like showing pictures of naked children to a pederast."

"Well, I bought a whole new set of workout clothes and I got a new full-year gym membership. But when I get there, it just seems so tedious somehow."

"I can't even clean up my apartment. Once a month I have to phone up my mother and have her do it for me. Otherwise it looks like a homeless squatter camp."

"It takes all my willpower just to get out of bed every morning and shave; that pretty much uses up my quotient for the day."

"I'm trying to be a writer. But mostly I've turned out to be a doodler. You should see the margins of my notebooks. All filled with little drawings, stick figures and so on. I don't know what made me think I could write. I'm actually a pretty good typist—I just can't think of anything to say."

SITUATION: You haven't kept up with your planned exercise routine. How do you tell your prey?

STIFF: "I suppose I could be doing a little more."

BOOR: "I've decided people who work out all the time are idiots."

CHARMER: "I had the best of intentions, I really did. But my problem was, just walking over to the gym tired me out, and by the time I was there, I was too tired to work out."

"I Find Myself Quite Boring, To Be Honest"

You're on a first date. You're just getting to know each other, but you realize that you've been talking about yourself a little bit too much. A good way to retract this impression of egotism and to allow your date to talk about herself is to tell her that you find yourself quite boring, and you'd rather talk about her.

Lean forward as if confiding a secret, and say, "You know what? I've heard all my own stories before. Many of them quite a few times, to tell the truth."

If your prey asks about you, reply, "Do we really have to talk about me? I'm so boring, and you're so interesting."

If your prey insists, give her the following capsule autobiography: "I was born, my parents brought me up, I graduated from high school, and now I work as an actuary. That's my life story. Now let's hear yours."

If she still insists on hearing more about you, well, then you have license to talk about yourself.

Charm is all about keeping our egos at arm's length.

SITUATION: After you've told an anecdote about yourself, your date tells you you're interesting.
STIFF: "Thank you."
BOOR: (jokingly) "Anyway, I've talked enough about me. Now let's hear what you think of me." But then he actually proceeds to go on even more about himself.

CHARMER: "I think the most interesting thing about me is that I'm a case study in being boring."

If You're Second Choice

If you are someone's second choice for boyfriend, team captain, companion, whatever, and you know it, there's nothing to do but cheerfully accept that role and make light of it.

First, acknowledge the fact: "I know Jim was your first choice, but that's okay. I don't mind being second choice, really. I'm used to it—it's pretty much the story of my life."

"It's actually sort of flattering to be somebody's second—usually, I'm third or fourth."

"Being second choice keeps me from getting a swelled head. Believe me, if I thought I was the favorite, I'd be insufferable."

Cheerfully say, "I do feel a little like the substitute teacher who gets no respect. People don't pay much attention to me, and they throw spitballs at me behind my back, but hey, substitute teachers exist for a reason—'cause we're better than nothing."

Raise your arms and cry out, "The second string is here! Hey, the varsity needs to rest from time to time."

"I'm here as the understudy, and believe me, given that this is my big chance, I'm going to give it my all. I'm like Avis. I try harder."

If you're second choice in a romantic context, say, "It's like that old song said—if you're not with the one you love, love the one you're with. Well, here I am."

"Maybe you can just close your eyes and pretend I'm Jim."

Make light of your second choice status gracefully enough, and soon you'll be first choice.

SITUATION: You ask a girl to the prom, and she inadvertently lets slip that she will go with you since her boyfriend just broke off with her.

STIFF: (meekly) "Oh. Okay."

BOOR: (angrily) "Forget it you bitch, now I don't want to go with you anyway!"

CHARMER: (lightly) "I feel sorry for you. I get to be with my first choice, you have to settle for second."

If He Doesn't Remember You

Unless you look like Orlando Bloom or Keira Knightley, you are fated to occasionally suffer the ignominy of not being remembered by someone you recently met. This is actually a wonderful opportunity to make a good impression, to show you have your wits about you and your ego in check. So when your prey—or anyone else—apologizes for not remembering you, just say:

"That's okay, really, I'm afraid I'm a very forgettable person."

"No problem, I just have one of those faces."

"It's okay. I'm used to it. To be honest, nobody ever remembers me."

"It's quite alright. I'm sure someone like you meets a lot of people, and you can't be expected to keep them all straight—especially a non-entity like me."

You must say all these things cheerfully. If any hint of self-pity creeps into your voice, the positive impression will sour. But ironically, if you do pull it off, you'll actually make yourself a memorable person, since you'll undoubtedly be the first person your prey has ever met who has had the presence of mind to say something like that.

SITUATION: Your prey—whom you met three days before—obviously doesn't remember you when you say hi. He apologizes. What do you say?

STIFF: "Oh, we met three days ago. Billy introduced us, remember?"

BOOR: "Yeah, well, the only reason I remember you is because of that big fucking zit on your nose."

CHARMER: "Don't worry about it. It's actually an advantage not to be very memorable, you know. If I ever decide to commit a crime, no

---

one will ever be able to describe me because I have no distinguishing marks and no distinguishing features."

Your Children

People are absolutely sick to death of hearing what little geniuses other people's children are. You can provide a pleasing contrast by disparaging your own.

Let's say your son swims competitively. Say, "My son is growing up to be a combination of Mark Spitz and Albert Einstein.... He's got Spitz's brains and Einstein's swimming ability."

"You know how some parents warn their children that they'd better study harder or otherwise they're going to become garbage collectors? I tell Johnny to study harder so that he can *become* a garbage collector."

Another rich vein to mine is how your children treat you. Most parents complain about the lack of respect they get, but they'll still be reassured to hear you get even less:

"My daughter actually introduces me to her friends by saying, 'This is my Dad. He's really annoying.'"

"The two things I hear from them most often are, 'Dad, shut up' and 'Dad, go away.' Sometimes I suspect I don't get the sort of filial piety I should."

"I never knew until I had kids that I'm just a walking, talking embarrassment."

SITUATION: Your son is on the baseball team.
STIFF: "Johnny is on the baseball team."
BOOR: "Johnny hit two home runs in one game a while back. Takes after his old man, I guess."
CHARMER: "Johnny had three errors in one game the other day. Takes after his old man, I guess."

The Whispered Aside

After you've done or said the right thing—as any charmer should do—it can be beneficial to have little contradictory confessions to share with your prey. So after you help the old lady across the street, whisper to your prey, "What I'd really like to do is shove the old biddy in front of a car." It's not as if you'd actually do that—after all, you've just done the opposite. But by saying something naughty, you've erased any taint of smugness from your good deed.

If your prey witnesses you lose a tennis match and then give your opponent a hearty handshake with the words, "The best man won," afterward whisper to your prey, "How obvious was it that I was lying?"

If your prey witnesses you make a donation to the local United Way, afterward grumble, "Buying a reputation for goodness can get pretty damn expensive."

The whispered aside needn't even follow a good deed. Little bits of gossip are always welcome. If you're walking through town with your prey and you happen to run into different people you know, each of whom you exchange warm greetings with, have a little nugget of information gift-wrapped for your prey about each: "We always greet each other like long lost brothers, but he'd just as soon see me dead." (It's okay to be a phony if you're a cheerfully self-acknowledged one.)

The impression you want to leave your prey with is that the two of you are co-conspirators in this silly game called Life.

SITUATION: Your prey witnesses you put a five-dollar bill into the Salvation Army bucket at Christmas time.

STIFF: "I guess it's a good cause."

BOOR: "You see that? That was a five, not a one. And by the way, I didn't see *you* putting any money in."

CHARMER: "I *tried* to pull some money out as I was putting the bill in, but couldn't."

"For Five Seconds There ..."

Another approach after doing or saying the right thing is to act surprised by your own behavior. It allows you to appear modest and underlines your nobility at the same time.

Let's say you've played a friendly—but trash-talking—game of tennis with your friend. After he beats you, you go to the net to shake his hand and tell him, "Congratulations, you deserved the victory. I don't seem to have an answer for your serve, and I can't scramble as well as you." As soon as the words are out of your mouth, do a double take and exclaim, "Wow—for about five seconds there, I was actually a good sport. Anyway, after an hour of trash-talking, five seconds of sportsmanship is all you get—so I hope you enjoyed it while it lasted."

After you hold a door open for somebody, shake your head and say, "What was *that*? I don't usually hold the door open for people. Hmm. I have to get back to being my rude self."

If you offer someone some of your meal, act mystified afterward. Say, "Well that was certainly a departure from my usual piggish self. I must have been in a fugue state or something."

After you do someone's laundry and fold it for them, say, "Hey—who hypnotized me? I wouldn't usually do that."

SITUATION: You've given your prey a ride to the airport, saving him the cost of a taxicab ride. As he's getting out, he thanks you profusely.
STIFF: "Oh, sure."
BOOR: (who probably wouldn't do this in the first place) "You owe me, man, you owe me big time."

CHARMER: "This is one of my very rare munificent moods. Don't know what's gotten into me—some evil spirit must have taken over my body."

When There's a Lull in the Conversation

The best thing to do with awkward silences, especially when you are on a date, is avoid them. (This is easily done by having stock questions like "What would you do if you won the lottery?" on hand.) But if a lull does occur, rather than let it become uncomfortable, it's best to jokingly draw attention to it.

Ask, "Was that what they call an awkward silence?"

Or say, "In case you hadn't noticed, I'm the strong, silent type … well, the silent type, anyway."

Or, "I can't believe *you and I* would run out of things to say," as if you and she are the last people in the world who would not have things to talk about.

You can always just blame yourself: "As you can see, I'm quite the conversationalist." (This gives her the opportunity to blame herself, allowing both of you to be gracious at the same time.)

Or use the opportunity to proffer a compliment: "I can't think of anything to say. I must be intimidated by your intelligence" (pick her most impressive quality).

Or say, "I bet silences bother you more than they do me. If you like, we can have a silence contest. Or a staring contest." This allows you to stare into each other's eyes, which always provides the illusion of intimacy.

Or just ask, "Do you find these silences awkward?" Her answer will actually be very revealing: she'll probably say no, in which case you know that you're with an average (or insensitive) woman. If, on the other hand, she admits that yes, they are a little awkward, you know you're with a more honest (and therefore more interesting) woman.

SITUATION: There is an awkward silence during your dinner date. How do you break it?

STIFF: "So ... how's your entrée?"

BOOR: "Boy, you're a real lump on a log."

CHARMER: "I'm not always this charming, you know. Sometimes I'm just quiet and boring."

"On the Internet …"

One way to humorously highlight your personal shortcomings is to compare yourself to the way you advertise yourself on the Internet.

For instance, if someone asks you how tall you are, reply, "Five foot eight." Then add brightly, "But *on the Internet*, I'm five eleven."

Or, "I weigh 220. But on the Internet, I'm 'a trim 185.'"

"I'm forty-five. But on the Internet, I'm only thirty-five."

"I flip burgers for a living. But on the Internet, I'm a doctor."

"My last vacation, I stayed with my brother in the Bronx. But according to my Web site, I like to vacation in the south of France."

"When I get some spare time, mostly I like to watch football or ultimate fighting on TV. But on the Internet, I like long walks on the beach."

"Most of my family is on welfare, and some of us deal a little blow on the side. But according to my Web page bio, I come from an old banking family."

A certain amount of resume padding is expected of everyone. But in this age of electronic romance, an absurd amount will strike your prey—who is probably guilty of a small amount of padding himself—as quite funny.

SITUATION: The subject of Internet dating sites arises.
STIFF: "I used one once."
BOOR: "I've never had any problem getting laid, and I've never had to use one of those sites." (In fact, he uses them all the time.)
CHARMER: "I actually put my brother's picture on my site. He's a lot better-looking than me. But if you'd never met me before, you might

---

just think that was a really good picture, taken before I'd put on some weight and lost a little hair."

PART IV
Recovering From a Faux Pas

Everyone, no matter how slick, commits social blunders from time to time. The key is to recover from them gracefully, which is usually done by bemoaning your error in some humorous fashion. In fact, if you can come back smoothly enough, you'll come across even better than had you not stumbled in the first place. This is not to suggest that you purposely make the errors described in this section. But the following chapters are worth studying, because as surely as you're reading this sentence, you'll need to recover from a faux pas at some point.

You can't just deny that you made a social mistake; this just compounds your error. But you needn't hang your head in shame and act mortified, either. To err is human; to poke fun at oneself afterward, divinely charming.

"I'm Shallow"

If you say something that makes you sound superficial, the best way to recover is to shrug, "I'm very shallow you know." Your prey will understand, because we're all superficial at times. (Who among us is immune to beauty?)

Explain, "Some people judge others by whether they're kind, thoughtful, and sensitive. I don't care about those things. With me, all that matters is whether you're good-looking and have money."

Say, "I'm a firm believer in judging a book by its cover." Take the opportunity to compliment your prey: "Hey, I wouldn't even be talking to you if you weren't so good-looking."

Continue, "When I say somebody's net worth is two million, it's not just an expression, I mean his *entire worth* as a human being."

"I am literally about an eighth of an inch deep."

Since anyone so aware of what shallowness is couldn't really be that way himself, by acknowledging the quality in yourself, you're showing you're just the opposite.

SITUATION: You've just said something superficial, and your prey gives you a mini-lecture about the importance of having good values.
STIFF: "I know."
BOOR: "Fuck off, good values are for losers."
CHARMER: "When people talk about having good values, I always figure they mean 'good value,' as in getting a lot for your money."

When You've Been Nasty

We all get nastier than we should from time to time. When that happens, we must own up to our own nastiness, and then show remorse, lest we be mistaken for truly evil. (Only villains admit to their own villainy with gleeful egotism.) So shake your head and say:

"Ouch—am I really that bitchy?"

"I seem to be full of poison and jealousy. No milk of human kindness here."

"You have to consider the source. By my standards, that was actually flattery—I'm usually much meaner."

"Malice, spite, and envy are the guiding lights of my personality."

"When I was born, a witch showed up and said that every time I spoke, a toad would come out of my mouth. I guess that's what she meant."

"Have you ever met a nastier person?"

"I'm a 'hater' alright."

SITUATION: You've just blurted out that you hope your worst enemy gets cancer and dies.
STIFF: "I guess I shouldn't have said that."
BOOR: "And I hope it's a slow, agonizing death."
CHARMER: "One of these days, I'm actually going to find something nice to say about somebody. Maybe I shouldn't, though, because the people who know me would probably have heart attacks."

You're the Bad Guy

If you slip up and do something bad—not charmingly naughty, but *bad*—you can mitigate the evil impression you've just made by immediately comparing yourself to a famous villain of literature or film.

If you've been selfish and arrogant, say, "I guess I'm a lot like that rich guy in *Titanic*."

If you've been mean, say, "My role model has always been that bully, Biff, in *Back to the Future*."

If you've installed a pirate cable box, say, "I'm like Professor Moriarty—the master criminal from Sherlock Holmes."

If you cackle gleefully at someone's misfortune, "Just call me the Wicked Witch."

If you've plotted someone's downfall, "My middle name is Cruella de Vil."

The ironic thing is, you actually did seem like those bad guys until you pointed it out. Don't make your bad guy too flattering. (At a certain level, all guys want to be the Jack Palance character in *Shane*.) The idea is to compare yourself to an evil buffoon, not an appealingly cool antihero.

This technique works not only for bad behavior, but for any sort of negative impression you might create: if you've just been rejected and are sexually frustrated, "I feel like that toothless guy in *Deliverance*."

Don't be afraid to use references from politics, either. ("Give me half a chance and I'd turn into Slobodan Milosevic.")

SITUATION: You've just playfully shoved your friend, causing him to unexpectedly trip and fall fairly hard on his rear end.
STIFF: "Oops, sorry."
BOOR: "You klutz!"
CHARMER: "You know, Hulk Hogan got a lot of his moves from me."

When Your Ego Shows

Sometimes, especially if you're male, the occasional boast will just come bursting out, despite your best intentions. (The male ego is a ravenous creature that needs constant feeding.) After you've blurted out some such comment, when the sour stench of your egotism hangs heavy, use one of these lines to clear the air:

"Oops. My ego just reared its ugly head again. I've got to keep that thing on a shorter leash."

"Sorry, I have the male curse—rampant egotism."

"A naked ego really is a hideously ugly thing, isn't it?"

"On my worst days, and this seems to be one of those, I can make Donald Trump look humble and unassuming."

"My need for self-affirmation is pathetic, isn't it?"

"I've got to stop boasting. I've got to stop boasting. I've got to stop boasting. My psychiatrist told me that if I say that three times after each boast, it'll cure me."

"My ego is like a second head attached to my shoulders—I don't want it, and it repulses people, but it's there, and there doesn't seem to be anything I can do about it."

"At home, I have a little shrine to myself."

If you have a typically male ego, it's best to memorize all these lines, since you'll have plenty of opportunity to use them.

SITUATION: You've just blurted out that you graduated from college Phi Beta Kappa.

STIFF: (slightly abashed) "No big deal, I guess."

BOOR: "I am so much smarter than most people, it's not even funny."

CHARMER: "The doctors said I have Tourette's Syndrome. But instead of swearing, I just burst out boasting. Really, it's totally beyond my control."

If You've Just Related an Accomplishment

If you've just boasted about something you did a while back, follow up by mentioning how pathetically proud you were at the time, and how foolish it all seems in retrospect. This will make you seem less conceited. (The mere fact that you can recognize your own conceit puts you way ahead of the pack.) So after you mention your Salesman of the Year award, add:

"My feet didn't touch the ground for forty-eight hours afterward. It was pretty pathetic."

"You would have thought I had just single-handedly fought off the Persians at Thermopylae."

"My head swelled so big I could barely fit through that door."

"At the time, I actually pretended to be modest about it ... boy was that ever false modesty."

"If pride is a sin, well, I was a pretty bad sinner."

"I'll tell you, it got so bad I started referring to myself in the third person. I was having delusions of grandeur left and right."

"I had egotism the way some people have bad body odor. I'm telling you, it really stunk."

"I became one of those guys who's so conceited he doesn't even realize how conceited he is."

The great thing about this technique is that it allows you to boast even more under the guise of making fun of yourself. ("My IQ is 163—see, I told you I'm conceited!")

SITUATION: You've just dropped the fact that you were once a final-ist for Miss Iowa.

STIFF: Realizing she's just boasted, she gives an involuntary little half shrug.

BOOR: "I should have won, too, but the bitch who won went around blowing everybody. How could I compete with that?"

CHARMER: "Once I started getting compliments about it, I started repeating those compliments to other people, which forced them in turn to compliment me." Makes a motion as if casting a reel, then adds, "My favorite sport became fishing for compliments. Hmm ... guess it still is."

"Thank You for Letting Me Boast"

Another way to clear the air after having boasted is to turn the focus to your prey's tolerance (as if he had any choice):

"Anyway, you're really gracious to let me go on like this."

"Thank you for your patience, most people would have told me to shut up long ago."

"Thank you for letting me talk about this."

"I must say, you have great forbearance."

"It's very good of you to at least pretend to be interested."

"Thanks so much for tolerating my egotism."

"You must be so sick of hearing me boast." (This offers your prey a chance to be gracious in turn.)

SITUATION: You've droned on for about three minutes about your glorious football career.

STIFF: "I guess I went on a little too long."

BOOR: (with a sigh) "I really was incredible."

CHARMER: "You seem to be one of the only ones who'll put up with my bragging. I do appreciate it."

If You've Been Caught Kissing Ass

There are some situations where a certain amount of toadying is unavoidable, whether it's with your boss, your customer, your in-laws, your spouse, or even someone you genuinely admire. In fact, much of this book is about how to kiss ass, because to the kissee it's generally a pleasant experience; it is only to the third party who witnesses it that it is so off-putting. So if your prey happens to be that witness, it's best to put a little distance between yourself and your behavior. As is usually the case, the best way to lessen the embarrassment is to point out what you've done.

Say, "Kissing ass just seems to come naturally to me."

Or, "Some people are born leaders." Shrug, "I'm a born follower."

"I hate myself. That's why I abase myself this way."

"I guess that was a pretty subservient performance. Seems my destiny is just to be a yes-man."

"Sorry, sometimes my servile nature just gets the better of me."

"I'm thinking about getting a tattoo: 'born to be a sycophant.'"

"My nickname is Obsequious Flatterer."

"Bowing and scraping are what I do best."

"It's bad enough to have acted that way, but it's really embarrassing that you had to see me."

Or, sarcastically, "I refuse to kiss ass. That is one thing I absolutely will not do."

Or explain why you have to butter that person up, then say, "But I still feel as if I have to take a shower afterward."

These comments will make your ass-kissing seem a temporary anomaly rather than the real you.

SITUATION: Your prey has just witnessed you toadying up to your boss.

STIFF: Looks away in embarrassment.

BOOR: "Listen, I hate the fucking guy as much as anyone, but I have to kiss his ass to keep my job."

CHARMER: "I think in a previous life I must have been a worm. Okay, okay ... in this life, too."

When You've Been Stupid

It happens to all of us. There are occasions when we just don't see things that are obvious to everyone else. Going along with the theory that you'll seem smarter by acknowledging your own errors, here are some lines to help you recover:

"Sometimes I have to be hit over the head with a two-by-four."

"Even *I'm* annoyed by my own stupidity sometimes."

"It was there under my nose the entire time, saying, 'Look at me,' and I still couldn't see it."

"I have to admit, if someone else had done that, I'd be ranting about how stupid he was."

"There's a brain buried in here somewhere. It takes a certain kind of intelligence to get everything wrong."

"My skull is the same size as other peoples', it's just my brain that's a lot smaller. Sometimes if I move too quickly, I can actually hear it rattle around in there."

"I'm not stupid, I'm just slow … Okay, I'm stupid."

"I must have been deprived of oxygen at birth or something."

If your prey is the one who pointed out your error, look at him in consternation and cry out, "This is why I hate talking to people who are smarter than me!"

SITUATION: You were the only one in your group who didn't see that an attractive "woman" was in fact a female impersonator.
STIFF: "Oh my god … I honestly couldn't tell."
BOOR: "How the hell was I supposed to know? She's better-looking than *your* girlfriend, that's for sure."

CHARMER: "I'm so dumb, I probably would've had a hard time telling even if he'd been completely naked."

If You've Overreacted

We all overreact at times, and, as a result, look temperamental. But you can keep yourself from being permanently enshrined in the Twit Hall of Fame with a little self-acknowledgment.

Start by saying, "Guess I overreacted a touch."

Or, "There's no excuse for me to act like such a twit. Guess I owe someone an apology."

"My specialty is creating tempests in teapots."

"That's pretty much the story of my life: much ado about nothing."

"I'm practicing for my role in an upcoming horror movie. I'm going to be the girl who screams when she sees the monster." (Say this even if you're a guy.)

"My middle name is Hysteria."

"It seems to fill a void in my soul to be melodramatic."

By making fun of your overreaction, you average out to a normal response.

SITUATION: It looks as if someone is about to ram into you with a large wooden crate he's carrying, but he sees you and manages to stop himself at the very last second. Nevertheless, you cry out, "Ow!" in anticipation of pain that does not materialize.

STIFF: (sheepishly) "I thought he was going to hit me."

BOOR: "Jesus, be careful, willya?!"

CHARMER: "It's a little known fact, but if you say 'Ow' loudly enough, you can actually ward off the impact."

If You've Been Caught in a Lie

If you've been caught lying, you can never recover entirely, but you can undo the damage a little.

If you sense early on that your prey sees through your lie, immediately react, before he can accuse you of dishonesty, "Why did I say that? That's not true."

But if you do get caught, say, "Sorry, I guess I shouldn't be playing these little games with you," as if harmless little games were all you were playing.

Then put the emphasis on his ability to see through you, taking it away from your dishonesty. Say, "I should have known, you're way too smart for me to try to fool."

"You have a great built-in bullshit sensor."

"You should work for the FBI."

"You're a human lie detector."

"You have a mind like a steel trap."

Shake your head, "Never scam a scammer." This effectively puts him at your level, but not in an insulting way. (People often *like* to think of themselves as operators.)

If you've lied about a nonexistent accomplishment, and you get caught: "You're so accomplished that it makes me feel as though I have to keep up with you. You're the only one who makes me feel that way." This makes you seem less of a habitual liar.

If you lied in order not to have to include your prey in some activity, one way out is to say, "I didn't want to put you on the spot by inviting you, since I knew you wouldn't want to go."

One comment you want to avoid is, "Well, there goes my credibility," because, while that describes what your prey's reaction *should* be, you don't want to encourage it.

SITUATION: You've just been caught in a lie by your prey.
STIFF: "Well, you caught me."
BOOR: "You trying to tell me you never lied?"
CHARMER: "You're a *mind reader.* I bet nobody gets *anything* by *you.*"

"I Don't Do Anything That's Not Calculated"

If someone calls you on an ulterior motive for anything you do, look him straight in the eye and make the above statement. Let's say you've just soundly thrashed your prey in a round of golf. He says, "The only reason you suggested going golfing was so you could show off what a good player you are." Reply, "Absolutely. Guilty as charged. As a matter of fact, there's a motive for everything I do. The reason I offered you a ride over here was so I could show off my new car."

Continue, "The only reason I brought up college was so you'd ask me where I went. The reason I took off my shirt wasn't because it was so hot—it was because I wanted to show off my muscles. Once you know how to read me, I'm pretty much an open book."

Your prey may respond with words to the effect of, "Ha! I knew it all along!"

Hold out your hands in a gesture of openness and say, "I was *only* trying to impress you. Is *that* so bad?" This should mollify your prey somewhat, and he should also appreciate your honesty—since most people never admit to such subterfuges.

If your prey still seems a little too triumphant about his being able to see through you, put him back on the defensive by saying, "The great thing was, you took the bait each time—you played golf, you rode in my car, and so on. That's what I like about you—I can always count on you."

SITUATION: Your prey says, "The only reason you suggested a game of chess was so you could show off."

STIFF: "No—I just enjoy chess!"

BOOR: "Nah, I just didn't realize you were going to suck so bad."

CHARMER: "You caught me. But you've got to realize—I only did it because you're so much better than me in everything else."

When You've Been Boring

If you've ever given a speech when a brief answer would have sufficed, a self-aware comment is called for:

"Anyone still awake?"

"I didn't actually talk for that long, it only seemed that way."

"Like to hear that one more time?"

"Anyway, and so on, ad nauseum, I guess."

"My motto is, never say in twenty-five words what can be said in two hundred and fifty."

"To me, brevity is a dirty word."

"Can I get anybody some coffee? How about smelling salts?"

"If anyone here suffers from insomnia, I'm selling tapes of myself talking for five dollars."

No matter how long you've gone on, if you end with a self-deprecatory comment about your verbosity, you'll leave an impression of charm.

SITUATION: You've just given a three-minute reply to your prey's question, two and three-quarter minutes longer than he wanted to hear.

STIFF: Makes up for his verbosity by answering the next few questions monosyllabically.

BOOR: (shaking his head) "Pearls before swine."

CHARMER: "My specialty is the filibuster."

When You've Repeated Yourself

We all have a certain stock of anecdotes and jokes that we trot out from time to time; inevitably, some will get repeated to the same person. If you're not sure your prey has heard a story before, it's safest to ask him at the outset. But if you forget and blunder through the entire thing, you must acknowledge the fact afterward:

"I've told you that story before, haven't I? And you're so polite, you just sat through the entire thing without saying a word."

"Next time, please stop me before I humiliate myself that way."

"Well, I guess you're becoming acquainted with the limits of my repertoire."

"I only have a few stories, so I have to milk them for all they're worth."

"I guess I'm a repeatee bird."

"The Alzheimer's is setting in early."

"Hey, I'm just getting warmed up. Expect to hear that joke two or three *more* times before I'm through."

The only thing you have to watch out for after you've told a story twice is to then also repeat one of these lines.

SITUATION: You tell your prey a joke. His pained smile alerts you to the fact that you've told him that same one before.
STIFF: "Oh—I guess I've told you that one before."
BOOR: "That's a good joke—worth hearing more than once."
CHARMER: "One of my special charms is that you get to hear all my jokes twice. And if you're really lucky, three times."

If You're Caught Looking in the Mirror

From time to time, people catch us looking in the mirror. This is always a little embarrassing, because the assumption—usually correct—is that we're admiring ourselves. The simplest way to cover up your vanity is to express dismay at what you see in the mirror: "Am I getting old!"

"I'm way past the point where young women give me a second look. Now even middle-aged women don't give me a second look."

Or say, "I'm thinking about getting plastic surgery to correct my many flaws ... Ah, but then I'd have to lie about it like everyone else."

Or just mock yourself. Whisper a barely audible "I love you," and blow the mirror a kiss.

Shrug, "Just call me Narcissus."

"You know, of all the great love stories in history ... Antony and Cleopatra ... Romeo and Juliet ... I think this one is actually the most intense." When your prey asks which one you're talking about, reply matter-of-factly, "You know, me and the mirror."

SITUATION: You're caught primping in front of the mirror. What do you do?

STIFF: Quickly runs his hand through his hair to make it look as if he had been making sure his hair wasn't too unkempt.

BOOR: Ignores prey, keeps primping.

CHARMER: "This is encouraging. Usually when I look in a mirror, it cracks."

The Greeting Kiss

There is no moment so consistently, ineffably awkward as the greeting kiss. First of all, there is the initial question of is-this-going-to-be-a-kiss-or-just-a-handshake as you move forward to greet your prey. You can usually take your cue from the body language of your prey. Once you realize that it's going to be a kiss, you must commit wholeheartedly. Hesitate, and your chance for gracefulness is lost.

Secondly, there is the question of whether to actually kiss your prey on the cheek, or just air kiss. (Generally, the air kiss is preferable—she doesn't want a big wet one planted on her cheek.)

Thirdly, you must determine if this is going to be a single kiss or a French-style double kiss. Take your cue here from the pretentiousness of your prey. (Pretentious = French-style.)

Fourth, how much body should you put into the hug, and how long should it last? The general rule here is, stand relatively straight as you do it (i.e., if you have to lean forward too much, it becomes awkward). Make it last a full second: if you let go first, you may seem somehow weak and unenthusiastic in your greeting. (By the way, hugs tend to go with single kisses; the French double kiss is rarely accompanied by a hug.)

Because this duet obviously calls for instantaneous reactions to subtle signals, it often—usually, in fact—turns into an orgy of mixed signals, missed calls, and all-around embarrassment. It is particularly hard because one is expected to sustain the requisite effusiveness throughout. (The old handshake was so much easier.)

SITUATION: You're about to greet your female prey (you're a male). She opens her arms wide.

STIFF: Hesitates at first, then spasmodically lunges forward to give her a kiss, missing her cheek and pecking her ear instead.

BOOR: Kisses her on the mouth and puts his hands on her hips instead of her shoulders.

CHARMER: Muffs the kiss and hug, but then says, "You know, this is one social ritual I always blow. Next time, can we just shake hands?"

If You Were Tongue-Tied

It happens to all of us: there are moments when the right words just won't come. Unfortunately, these times tend to occur when you least want them to. Should your prey happen to witness such muteness on your part, this is what to say afterward:

"I always get that deer-in-the-headlights response. Just lucky, I guess."

"Freezing up is one of my specialties."

"In case you were wondering, that was me at my most eloquent."

"I always come up with the perfect response—half an hour later."

"Whenever it matters most, my mind always manages to go blank."

"The French have a term, 'sangfroid,' to describe somebody with nerves of steel, which translates literally as 'cold-blooded.' I guess that makes me hot-blooded."

"At least you can't accuse me of being glib."

"You know how some people have silver tongues? I have a lead one."

"I wasn't showing restraint there. I just couldn't think of anything to say. My tongue was literally tied in a knot."

By making a joke of your ineloquence, you can actually turn it into the opposite.

SITUATION: A coworker gives you an unexpected and undeserved tongue-lashing, then stomps off in a huff. You're too stunned to respond. What do you say afterward to your prey, who witnesses all this?

STIFF: "That's not true—that wasn't my fault."

BOOR: "What an asshole!"

CHARMER: "I wasn't exactly given the gift of gab, was I? I guess I was given the gift of silence instead. That's highly underrated, you know."

PART V
Deference

Aretha Franklin probably phrased it best when she said she wanted R-E-S-P-E-C-T. It's what all of us want. And there's no better way to give it to your prey than to put him above you, in whichever arenas self-respect is measured. So go ahead and elevate him by being deferential.

Keep in mind that your emphasis here should always be on his attributes, not your lack of them. (The better you are, the better it makes him.)

All of the sections up to this one have consisted of advice for both sexes, for use on both sexes. This section is primarily for males, for use on other males. Males are pathetically competitive creatures, forever trying to prove that they are superior at just about everything. So indulge your prey by artfully deferring to him. If you succeed at this, you will be the real victor.

One Downmanship

Obnoxious people play one upmanship; charmers do the opposite. One downmanship takes two basic forms: when your prey boasts, and when he is self-effacing.

If he says his golf handicap is a twelve, even if yours is a four, tell him it's an eighteen.

If your prey boasts about his annual income, even if you make that much in a month, ruefully intone, "I'm just a piker by comparison."

The principle here is simple: he wants admiration. Give it to him.

A self-effacer, on the other hand, is an example of misery wanting company, company even more miserable than he. So if your prey complains about how he's almost broke, tell him you're deep in debt yourself.

When your prey complains that he hasn't gotten laid in months, even if you have a harem at your disposal, reply, "That's nothing. I haven't gotten laid in a year." He'll feel like a lothario by comparison.

Your prey may complain about being out of shape. Even if your resting heart rate is forty-eight and you have 6 percent body fat, tell him that your doctor recently informed you that you'll die within a few years if you don't change your lifestyle.

If your prey is married, he probably complains about his wife. Make yours sound like a cross between Imelda Marcos and Lorena Bobbitt.

If your prey complains that he is unpopular, you're about to be tarred and feathered.

You get the idea. You're never as accomplished, and always worse off.

SITUATION: Your prey proudly mentions that he bench-pressed three hundred pounds.
STIFF: "Is that good?"
BOOR: "That's nothing. My own cousin can bench four-twenty."
CHARMER: "The other day, I benched a hundred pounds three times. Same thing, right?"

"You're Like Catnip for Women!"

Telling another guy he is very attractive to women is the compliment he most wants to hear. And nothing makes the compliment seem more sincere than bemoaning your own lack of success with the opposite sex at the same time.

"Man, you could have any woman you want!" pretty much sounds like the keys to heaven.

"I bet your biggest problem is how to get rid of them all afterward. Do you have an unlisted phone number? I bet even then you'd have to change *that* from time to time."

"What's it like to have the fish jump out of the water and into your boat?"

Express frustration: "A guy like you probably has no idea how hard it is for a guy like me to get girls."

"These women are just begging you to be friendly, and you just ignore them. Do you have to be hit over the head with a two-by-four?"

"I guess you don't think a woman is actually available unless she bellows, 'Hey sailor, over here!' and pulls up her shirt."

"If I looked like you, I'd work as a gigolo." (No man can resist the idea that women would pay to have sex with him.)

If your prey is the least bit grounded, he'll realize that he's not what you're making him out to be. Nonetheless, this kind of talk allows him to indulge at least temporarily in the kind of pleasant fantasy that we all like to lose ourselves in from time to time.

SITUATION: The talk turns to your prey's love life.
STIFF: "Do you … date much?"
BOOR: "I don't picture you cutting any wide swath."
CHARMER: "You seem to attract them like flies to honey. Does seducing girls ever get boring for you?"

His Strength

If your prey is a physical specimen, it never hurts to belabor that fact.

If he comes by his strength without working at it, say, "~~You~~ must ~~spend a lot of time weight-lifting~~." It will give him a little zing of pleasure to deny it. (It's always preferable to inherit wealth than to have to work for it.) Marvel, "I'd give anything to be that strong. Christ, I'd be happy just to *look* that strong."

Say, "You must be on steroids!" (If you suspect that he actually is, avoid the subject.)

Tell your prey, "I wish I had as much testosterone going through my system as you do. Guys like me always have to go around proving their masculinity, whereas you can just calmly sit back and feel secure, because nobody would ever doubt your masculinity."

"I bet the football coaches must have really drooled over you in high school." If he played football, ask if he ever put the shot or threw the discus, in a tone that indicates complete assurance that had he tried, he could have set the world record in either one.

Add, "I feel like a girl next to you. You ever think about trying out for that World's Strongest Man competition?"

Shake your head. "You look like one of those professional wrestlers. Thank goodness you don't act like one." If he can take a joke, add, "Well, most of the time."

Ask, "When you were a baby, did you have to strangle a large snake when it came into your crib, the way Hercules did?"

Your prey needn't actually be a powerhouse for you to flatter him this way; he must just think he is. But he must be stronger than you, otherwise he'll think you're mocking him.

If someone else is present, point at your prey and say, "This is my bodyguard. You wanna get to me, you gotta go through him!"

Or just ask the third person, "Ever notice how you never see Brian and Superman at the same time?"

SITUATION: Your prey attempts some feat of strength and fails.
STIFF: "I probably couldn't do that either."
BOOR: "Hah! You weakling!"
CHARMER: "Okay, who's got the Kryptonite?"

"How Am I?"

When your tall and handsome prey greets you by asking how you are, answer, "Same way I always feel when I'm around you—short and ugly."

Tailor your comments to whatever his strengths and your relative weaknesses are. Some other possible answers might be:

"Same way I always feel when I'm around you—fat and awkward."

"… slow and charmless."

"… unsuccessful and unsophisticated."

"… shabbily dressed and poorly groomed."

The combinations and permutations are endless.

Simply answer the query—to which he doesn't *really* want a response—by telling him how you are, and by extension, what *he* is—which is what he *does* want to hear.

SITUATION: Your prey has just greeted you by asking how you are.
STIFF: "Fine thanks, and you?"
BOOR: "Don't tell me you give a shit."
CHARMER: "Same way I always feel around you—poor and stupid."

"You're a Born Leader"

Leadership is one of those intangible qualities that many people think they have. The control freak thinks he has it because he likes to tell people what to do. The tantrum-thrower thinks he has it because people learn to not cross him. The liar thinks he has it because he can get people to believe things that aren't true. In fact, real leadership is one thing, and one thing alone: having people *want* to follow you. But all sorts of people see themselves as leaders.

So no matter what type your prey is, tell him:

"I'd follow you anywhere."

"You're a natural leader. You just come across commanding, like a general on the battlefield."

"You're a born leader. I just hope in the future you use your power for good rather than for evil." (This sounds like a doubtful compliment, but most people love power so much they'll just be flattered.)

"You should be president. You'd make a better president than [the current one], that's for sure."

"I feel like I'm with Captain Kirk of the Starship Enterprise." Stand at attention, click your heels, and salute him.

If you have occasion to correct him on anything, add, "For a moment there, I lost faith in you. Forgive me, I don't know how it happened, or why. It'll never happen again, believe me."

Many who crave power often achieve it, simply because they'll do anything to get it. They are, of course, not real leaders. Nonetheless, these are the type with whom this type of flattery works best.

SITUATION: Your prey suggests taking an alternate route to a party so as to avoid a certain section of town because it's dangerous.
STIFF: "You think so?"
BOOR: "Who died and left you in charge?"
CHARMER: "When I'm with you, I feel like I'm fighting in the jungles beside Che Guevara. I'll go where you lead."

"You're the Alpha Male Around Here"

Every guy likes to think of himself as an alpha male. So let your prey think that as well. If he in fact *is* one, you're making him more secure in his position; if not, he'll be all the more happy to hear it.

Say, "Maybe you could give me lessons some time on being dominant."

"Being around you really does drive home the fact that I'm a beta male."

"Sometimes it occurs to me to stand up to you, but somehow I always end up acceding to your superior force of will."

Say, "If this were a movie, you'd be played by Russell Crowe and I'd be played by David Spade."

"Just think of me as your personal assistant."

"I'm sort of like your valet."

"I'm sort of like Sancho Panza to your Don Quixote."

"You're the star of this show. I'm just a supporting player."

Address him as "captain" or "hitter." If he calls you, answer, "Yes sir," (but not sarcastically).

If you're roommates, say, "You're sort of the lord of the manor and I'm sort of the houseboy."

SITUATION: Your prey tells you that you're the alpha male in the area.
STIFF: (confusedly) "What? You really think so? I—I don't think so."
BOOR: "True."
CHARMER: "Nonsense. I'm honored just to be your sidekick."

The Tough Guy

The extent to which guys will go, and the risks they'll take in order to prove they're tough are often downright stupid. To those of us whose egos aren't tied up in that particular quality, it seems silly and even self-destructive. But, for better or worse—mostly worse—that's the way many guys are. Given which, it is better to fawn than scoff.

If your prey gets in fights, comment, "It must be great to know you can beat up any guy you meet. Remind me never to make you angry."

Add, "You know, you have to be careful, one of these days you're just going to cripple someone." Rather than inject a cautionary note, this will probably spark a pleasant reverie in your prey's mind in which he stands, Tarzan-like, beating his chest and letting out a jungle cry over his lifeless foe.

The Macho Man is flattered by comments that other people would find insulting—for instance, "I'd hate to run across you in a dark alley."

If your prey admits to some weakness, respond, "I'll tell you one thing—I'm not going to be the guy who makes fun of you for it."

If he's macho, there's a good chance he's into extreme sports. So give him the feedback he wants and tell him you'd be way too scared to hang glide/mountain bike/motocross race/ski jump/etc.

The people who will be the most pleased by this type of flattery are not real tough guys (who usually care little about being tough), but the wannabes, who care a great deal. Even if you feel nothing but contempt for this ersatz tough guy, you can at least amuse yourself by watching him preen as you compliment his manliness.

SITUATION: Your prey describes his recent parachute jump.
STIFF: "You could have gotten hurt."
BOOR: "Sounds like a big waste of time to me."
CHARMER: "There really are very few people brave enough to do that. You must not have any nerves."

Flatter Him in the Most Sincere Way

If you imitate your prey, he'll know that you admire him beyond all doubt. So go ahead and flatter him that way.

If he wears a pair of blue jeans and a white sweatshirt one day, put on a similar outfit the next day.

If he buys a certain style of shoes, buy a similar pair.

If he gets a haircut, get one yourself the next day.

If he has certain phrases he favors, employ them in his presence.

If he accuses you of imitating him, sheepishly admit guilt: "I can't help it. It sounds good when you say it, so I thought I would as well."

Your prey may not be observant enough to notice all these things; if so, point it out to him: "You looked so sharp in that outfit yesterday, I wanted to wear it today. Problem is, it doesn't look as good on me."

You don't want to do this so that people other than your prey notice, lest they think you a secondhand personality. But you do want to do it so that your prey notices. The thought you want to leave him with is, "I must be his hero."

If imitation is the sincerest form of flattery, then the ultimate flattery is to actually want to *be* somebody. Tell him, with envy in your voice if not your heart, "Man, I would love to lead your life. You have got to be the luckiest guy I know." Add, as if it's an afterthought, "Not that what you've accomplished is due to luck."

If things haven't been going his way, say, "What are you complaining about? The world is your oyster. Look at you." (Add a few specifics here if you can.) "Now stop whining and just be glad you are who you are. Think about it, things could be a lot worse. You could be me."

Tell your prey he's the envy of your set: "I know so many guys who are jealous of you, it's incredible. It seems like everyone around here just wants to be you." This is a compliment he will remember for a long time.

Add, "Ever notice how when you stand a certain way, a lot of guys will imitate your posture, or when you use a certain phrase, it'll find its way into the vocabulary of the other guys?" Your prey may have never noticed this for the very good reason that it never happened—but that won't keep him from taking you at your word.

There are few things more satisfying than knowing that others wish they were leading your life. Provide your prey that illusion, and you will put him into an egotistical trance, which is fairly close to nirvana.

SITUATION: You and your prey are talking about your lives.
STIFF: "You seem to be doing okay."
BOOR: "Man, you couldn't pay me enough to lead your life."
CHARMER: "There's only a very short list of guys I'd trade lives with. Maybe Warren Beatty, Mick Jagger, Wilt Chamberlain, Pablo Picasso, and you."

"Someone Like You"

One way of indirectly flattering your prey is to say how proud you are of a certain accomplishment, even though it would be nothing to a guy like him. This puts him on an altogether different level than yourself, and says, by implication, that since you are proud, he should be *extremely* proud.

Say, "I made five thousand dollars in the stock market last month. To someone like you, that's nothing, but to me, that's a lot of money."

Once your prey has been placed in such an exalted position, it's much easier for him to praise you; he will undoubtedly respond by saying, "Oh no, five thousand dollars is a lot of money for me, too. Congratulations." This allows him to not only feel like a big success, but gives him the opportunity to act humble and magnanimous as well. You've managed to get your boasting in without making him feel the need to one-up you. And you don't even seem that boastful because you couched your boast in relative terms.

Or say, "I'm so excited, I got a date with this really beautiful girl for Friday night. For a man of the world like you, that would be no big deal, but for a guy like me, this is a momentous event!"

Your prey will be tickled that someone—besides him—acknowledges the yawning gap between him and mere mortals.

Nothing will stroke someone's ego quite as effectively as being informed that he's big time.

SITUATION: You've just gotten an award. How do you tell your prey?

STIFF: "Sorry to boast, but I was just named Journalist of the Year for Russell County, Oklahoma."

BOOR: "Hey, I just got named Journalist of the Year. Of the *year!* Bet you'd like to get an award like that some time."

CHARMER: "This is almost embarrassing to relate to a guy like you, but ..."

"I Hate People Who ..."

The best way to compliment your prey who, say, just set a school record in the 800-meter run, is to tell him how much you hate people who can run that distance in a minute and fifty-seven seconds. This accomplishes several things all at once: First, you're complimenting him for his accomplishment. Second, it's a roundabout way of saying that you like him (otherwise you wouldn't feel comfortable phrasing your statement that way). Third, you've admitted that you're jealous of him—putting him in the superior position. And fourth, by actually telling him that you're jealous, you've made it clear that you're not resentful—for when envy is tinged with resentment, it's rarely admitted to.

So go ahead and tell your prey what he wants to hear: "Did I ever tell you how much I hate people who get 800s on their SATs?"

"... who have size thirty-two waists?"

"... who feel no need for either coffee or cigarettes?"

And so on. He'll love you for it, since there's no pleasure more exquisite than sparking jealousy.

SITUATION: Your prey has offered you a ride in his new car, a Mercedes, and you've just gotten in.
STIFF: "Nice car."
BOOR: "My experience is, people who drive Mercedes are assholes. How much this thing cost you?"
CHARMER: "Did I ever tell you how much I hate people who can afford these things?"

Talk about What a Lousy Lover You Are

What's even more damning than talking about how you've been impotent is to talk about how you get bad reviews in bed even when you do perform. Guys always love to hear this; it makes them feel quite the stud by comparison. (If you're with a woman who's a prospect, it's best not to go here.)

Tell your prey, "I was on a date with this new girl the other night, and the first time we did it, I could only last for ten seconds. That was really embarrassing. I redeemed myself later on though; the second time I lasted for a good thirty seconds."

"Foreplay is overrated. I figure if intercourse is enough for me, it should be enough for her."

Confide in your prey, "You know, I think the whole concept of the female orgasm is a myth."

"Just one time, I'd like to have a girl tell me I was good in bed. Usually when I ask if it was good for them, they say something like, 'Oh, you're a nice guy,' or something like that. Once when I was in bed with a girl, right afterward she masturbated right in front of me, saying she needed satisfaction, too."

"Another time, right after I finished making love to this other girl, she ran to the bathroom and threw up. Afterward she denied it, but I could hear her."

"The worst is when they get angry at you." Shudder, "I don't even want to talk about that."

"Several of my girlfriends have complained about me only wanting to do it twice a week."

"Once I've had sex, I'm done till at least the next day. I think these guys who say they can do it more than once in a day are lying."

If you really want to prove your low sex drive, say, "What's happened a couple of times is that I've started laughing at the wrong moment. I mean, the whole thing just struck me as so absurd. There we were with our clothes off, we must have looked so funny. I mean, when you think about it, sex really is a pretty ridiculous thing."

Conclude, "Sex is so overrated. I mean, it's okay, but I'm just not all that interested. Some guys seem to be really driven by it, but to me it's like a mild itch that I can do perfectly well without scratching, and to tell the truth, sometimes I go for weeks without even being itchy."

By the time you're through, you'll probably have made your prey feel like the studliest guy on earth. At the very least, you'll have made him feel that he's not alone.

SITUATION: You're telling your prey about a recent sexual incident at Club Med.
STIFF: "I got lucky, I guess."
BOOR: "That babe was crazy about me. Hey, when I screw a girl, she *knows* she's been screwed."
CHARMER: Shrugs, "I'm good at getting girls into bed. I'm just no good at keeping them. Once they've been to bed with me, they never seem to want to do it a second time."

"That's A Good Question"

If your prey throws you a curveball question that leaves you nonplussed, you can regain your equilibrium and compliment him at the same time by turning the focus onto his question. Simply respond by telling him what a good question he's asked.

If you need even more time to recover, say, "Your question has really thrown me for a loop."

Or, "That's such a tricky question, I'm not even sure how to answer that. You must be a great debater."

"You have a knack for asking the most difficult questions...."

Likewise, if your prey points out a flaw in your thinking, and you blurt out the first excuse that comes to mind, you'll look lame as well as stupid. So instead of either arguing or even admitting your own stupidity, turn the focus onto him. Positive comments about his comment are always welcome:

"That's a great suggestion."

"As always, you cut right to the heart of the matter."

"I should have known I could count on you to analyze the situation accurately."

"You're very insightful."

SITUATION: After you finish outlining a plan, your prey points out an obvious flaw you hadn't thought of.

STIFF: "Oh ... That's true, I guess."

BOOR: "Don't you think I already thought of that? I was going to get to that!"

CHARMER: "That's a very good point. A *very* good point."

"I'm Nobody"

It's common practice these days to Google somebody after meeting him, to find out what you can about him. If your prey has an entry, or multiple entries, and you have none (we've all Googled ourselves), make the following speech the next time you see him:

"I have a confession to make: I Googled you after meeting you. I'm so impressed that you've run so many 5Ks [or whatever it is that he's been listed for]. Now if you Google me, you'll find a lot of John Smiths. Unfortunately, none of them are me. That's because I'm a nobody. I'd *like* to be a somebody, like you. Maybe I should claim to be the John Smith who was born in 1743 and died in 1797; at least he got listed. Actually, there's a guy by my name who's listed who's supposed to be a prominent photographer. Maybe I'll claim to be him. Only problem is, he's got a different middle initial. But I don't think most people would notice that, do you?"

"It must be great to be important enough to be listed on the Net. I guess my only problem is, I've just never done anything worth mentioning. You're the kind of guy whose obituary will probably run in the big city newspapers. Me, I'll probably just be put in an unmarked grave."

SITUATION: You've Googled somebody after meeting him. What do you say the next time you see him?
STIFF: Nothing, because he's too embarrassed to admit he did it.
BOOR: Nothing, because he doesn't want to give him the satisfaction of knowing he did so.

CHARMER: "I was so impressed when I met you that I knew I'd be even more impressed if I Googled you, and sure enough, there you were, larger than life, with more listings than I could read."

PART VI

Being Cool

Some people are just naturally cool, and nothing fazes them; the rest of us must pretend. This is perhaps the hardest act to pull off, because it requires conquering your emotions. It is virtually impossible not to get angry when you've been insulted; but if you can pretend not to be, you'll come across cool. And if you act this way, you may find yourself actually getting less angry.

Remaining totally unaffected when someone else is raging is by far the most eloquent way of saying that you simply don't care enough about them to be upset by their opinions. If you can demonstrate this sort of nonchalance in front of your prey (preferably to a third party rather than to him), he will think you the ultimate in cool.

There are a couple chapters in this section about overcoming your fear. You never know when you'll be called upon to pretend courage, since scary situations can be hard to anticipate. And our nerves have a way of acting up just when we least want them to. But if you can act as if you don't have them, people will be impressed.

Be assured, cool will always be in fashion. (And although being cool is a trait that males aspire to more, for that reason, it is all the more devastating when exhibited by a woman.)

Roll With the Punches

When we're insulted, our instincts are to deny and lash back. A far better tactic is to agree with the insult, and even take it one step further. By showing that the insult doesn't faze you, you prevent it from stealing your dignity. (Others can rob you of your dignity only if you let them.)

If somebody calls you stupid, and you respond, "I am not! I'm smarter than you, you moron," you come across brittle. It also appears that the issue of intelligence is a sensitive one for you (i.e., you really are dumb). So, agree with your insulter instead: "It's true. I actually am borderline retarded."

Then lightheartedly sing the Scarecrow's song from *The Wizard of Oz*: "I could while away the hours, conferring with the flowers, if I only had a brain …" You'll find that not only will you maintain your dignity this way, you won't feel as bad about the insult. You'll naturally want revenge, but hold your counsel. Simply file away the insult, and at a later date, when your insulter inevitably makes a mistake himself, just say, "You *were* the one who called *me* stupid, weren't you?"

If someone tells you you're conceited, shrug and agree. "You're right. My ego is like an impregnable fortress that is impervious to facts."

If someone calls you a wimp, just shrug, "That's why I only fight girls—guys hit back."

If some boor tells you you're ugly, rather than recoil, just say, "It's true. My face was used as the prototype for a Halloween mask." You will not only retain your dignity by showing you're totally unaffected, you'll show that you are the bigger person. Later on, have your revenge served cold.

You can reply to any insult by saying, "You're right—but don't tell anyone, okay? I really don't want it getting around."

In fact, if you can think of the most wounding thing that anybody has ever said to you, and repeat it laughingly with a rueful acknowledgment that it's true, you'll come across quite self-assured.

SITUATION: Someone tells you you're a failure in life.
STIFF: "How dare you?"
BOOR: "Hey, I'd rather be me than an asshole like you!"
CHARMER: (calmly) "Am I ever. I'm surprised you're not embarrassed to be seen with me."

"You Hurt My Feelings ..."

If your prey—or anyone else—says something deliberately wounding, another great way to show you're unaffected is to act mock hurt. The easiest way to pull this off is to imagine you're dealing with a five-year-old (more often than not, you will be—emotionally if not chronologically). After all, would you really be hurt by anything a five-year-old said?

So put your hand over your heart and open your mouth as if in shock, then use a mild-but-exaggerated tone as you give voice to any combination of the following lines:

"Wow! You are really mean!"

"I can't believe you said that!"

"Have I done anything to deserve that type of treatment?"

"Don't you think I have any feelings?"

"I think I'm going to cry." (Use this one only if you're obviously not.)

You will simultaneously show that your prey's insult registered, giving him satisfaction, and that you really weren't affected by it.

SITUATION: Your prey has just told you that nobody at school likes you.
STIFF: (recoiling) "What?"
BOOR: (livid) "You think people like you, you piece of shit?"
CHARMER: (with exaggerated concern) "Why don't you just cut my heart out and feed it to the crows? I can't believe how cruel you are."

"That Doesn't Make Me a Bad Person"

If you're bad at anything, and your prey calls you on it, rather than argue the point, reply in an innocent, childlike voice, "Well ... that doesn't make me a bad person." This is such a pathetic reply that your prey's antipathy—and disgust with your performance—should immediately dissolve in laughter.

Let's say you've just raced your prey in a crossword puzzle contest, and by the time he finished the puzzle you had only gotten the answers to three clues. If he scoffs at your performance, or even if he doesn't, say in that childlike tone, "Just because I'm *dumb*, that doesn't make me *evil*, you know."

After you stink up the court in a tennis match, offer, "Just because I'm bad at tennis doesn't mean I'm not a nice person."

Likewise, "I may not be very good at reading maps, but I still have a good heart."

SITUATION: You've just gone on a planned five-mile jog with your prey, but had to stop after one mile because you were too winded. You meet up again, and your prey tells you you've got no guts.
STIFF: "I'm just out of shape, I guess."
BOOR: "I don't have to take shit like that from someone like you!"
CHARMER: (jokingly) "Just because I'm a little wimpy, that doesn't decrease my value as a human being."

Stay Calm

It is a law of physics that you cannot be hysterical and charming at the same time. Even if you feel like losing your temper or having a nervous breakdown, remain an icebox on the outside. Someone who stays level-headed while others panic inspires confidence. And if you can stay cool while all about you are losing their heads, it will add a certain heroic quality to your charm.

Case in point. The fire alarm at your school or office has gone off, and the smell of smoke informs you that it's not just another drill. Yet the line in the stairwell is not moving, leaving you trapped on the seventh floor. Instead of screaming at people to move, toss off a light-hearted line: "Now I know how Joan of Arc felt."

You and your prey have just gotten into a car accident. No one was hurt, but everybody is in a slight state of shock. Instead of yelling furiously at the other driver, turn to your prey and calmly say, "You know, I always wanted to try Demolition Derby."

A minor earthquake hits, and panic is in the air. Calmly hold up one finger and say, "The gods must be angry." If your prey asks you why, shrug, "Why do you think? We're living in a latter day Sodom and Gomorrah."

Most movies feature a hero, a villain, a trusted friend, a romantic interest, and a designated ninny. It is the job of the villain to act silky smooth and arrogant when he's not being cold-bloodedly sadistic. It is the job of the trusted friend to warn the hero of impending danger, then to die off early on. It is the job of the romantic interest to be beautiful and brave, and to not like the hero at first, but then to be won over by him. It is the job of the hero to act heroic and toss off bon mots even when his life is in danger. And it is the job of the designated ninny to complain and act hysterical, all of which serve better to counterpoint the hero's heroism.

Now ask yourself, which role do you want? (For purposes of this book we'll assume you're not a villainous multinational tycoon with scores of thugs at your disposal and world domination in mind.) If you find yourself getting hysterical, like it or not, you may be playing the role of the designated ninny.

It's one thing to be cool when there's nothing to be scared of, but when you're in an emergency and can still toss off a witticism—then you're James Bond.

SITUATION: You've gone camping with two buddies in Skamania County, Washington. It's gotten dark and all three of you are sitting around a campfire. Suddenly, a nine-foot-tall, eight-hundred-pound Sasquatch appears at the edge of the clearing, glaring at you.
STIFF: "Oh my God! We're going to die!"
BOOR: "Where's my rifle? I'm gonna bag that sucker!"
CHARMER: "Well hello there, big buddy. You remember to bring the marshmallows?"

Alcohol

It's hard to be charming when you're nervous. When you're tense, you can never react quickly with the right words: your very tenseness prevents them from flowing.

One way to overcome a bad case of nerves is to have a drink. The impression that alcohol makes us more charming is partly illusion, but it's partly real, based on the fact that we become more relaxed. Alcohol can actually turn a stiff into a charmer. (It can also make a boor really intolerable, but if you're a boor, you're probably not reading this book anyway.)

Do keep in mind, however, that while the alcohol will make your inhibitions evaporate, so it will do the same to your brains, to the tune of approximately eight IQ points per drink (the author made this number up, but it seems about right). This is why stumbling drunks always come across like idiots. And if it's hard to be charming when you're tense, it's impossible when you're vegetative. (Have you ever met someone who was really blotto whom you considered charming?) This is why so many police reports say that alcohol was involved—and why the Breathalyzer was invented.

You also don't want to get in the habit of consuming alcohol, otherwise that stupidity becomes permanent.

SITUATION: You're at a party where alcohol is being served.
STIFF: Abstains, his mother's warnings about killing brain cells echoing in the back of his head. Is slightly smug about being a teetotaler.
BOOR: Takes advantage of the open bar to have eight drinks. Tries to get palsy-walsy with almost everyone he sees. When he feels his

---

overtures have been rebuffed brusquely, picks a fight. Afterward vomits on the rug.

CHARMER: Has one or two drinks, just enough to banish his inner stiff, and proceeds to make himself enjoyable company—while simultaneously enjoying himself.

Show Perspective

Demonstrating that you can step outside yourself and view yourself with perspective always serves to convince people that you don't take yourself too seriously.

If the subject of history comes up, however obliquely, say, "I'm just a product of my times. I know how to get online and use my cell phone, but put me in the forest and I'd be helpless."

If describing a confrontation, don't say, "I was so pissed …" Say instead, "To my surprise, I found myself getting angry …" as if you're the type who can observe his own reactions with detachment.

If you have some bad luck, shrug it off with, "It's not the greatest tragedy that's happened in the history of mankind."

If a girl turns you down, take her point of view: "Why would she be interested in someone like me? I'm just an ugly guy with no money."

Or, "I'm just a stiff with a chip on his shoulder." This shows that in fact you are neither.

If you've just lost half your money in the stock market, point out, "At least I have a roof over my head and food to eat."

If referring to a setback you've experienced, say, "It seems silly to relate it now, but I thought the world was coming to an end."

If you're relating a story about a dangerous situation, say, "I thought I was going to have a heart attack right there. Thinking back on it, it really was pretty funny."

If you're showing your prey your place of work, whisper, "I don't really know what I'm doing, but I can fake it okay, and that's all you ever need to do to get by."

The impression you want to leave is that you are amused—though not particularly emotionally vested in—the ups and downs of your own life, and that what you are most amused by are your own foibles. (This is the essence of charm.)

SITUATION: Your prey has stopped by your office to drop something off.
STIFF: "Well, this is where I work."
BOOR: "I've done so much for this company, they oughta have a statue of me out in the front hall."
CHARMER: "This is where I pretend to be a grownup. It gets a little wearying, trust me."

Don't Try Too Hard to Prove Your Masculinity

Too many guys spend an inordinate amount of energy trying to prove to their buddies that they're heterosexual. You may have succumbed to this sort of peer pressure yourself. The problem is, trying too hard just makes you look insecure, not masculine. It also makes you look a bit stupid.

In fact, there is nothing more masculine than not worrying about appearing masculine. Real tough guys never feel the need to prove their toughness, and real studs never worry about how studly they appear. So the key to appearing confident is to simply relax.

This takes some restraint. If a group of guys starts raving about how attractive a certain girl is, but you don't find her so, don't be afraid to say it. Just shrug and say, "Not my type." If anyone thinks you're gay, so what? The only guys who really care about your sexual orientation are guys who want to have sex with you, and they don't particularly want to hear about how much you want some woman either.

Ironically, one of the most macho-sounding things you can say to your buddy under these circumstances is, "Ugh. I'd rather do you."

Another ironically macho-sounding comment during an argument with your buddy is, "If I'm wrong, I'll crawl around this entire stadium on my hands and knees and then blow you in front of everybody." (Don't worry, he won't take you up on it.)

If you know a gay man, don't be afraid to talk to him in front of the guys. Apart from the fact that it's rude not to, it will make you appear secure.

If you must, mention a girlfriend, but don't make too big a deal about her. Mention her only in context, and only in passing. (Some guys repetitively invoke "my girlfriend" like a mantra, to convince others of their heterosexuality.)

The overall message of this book is definitely *not* "to thine own self be true" (since charm comes naturally to so few of us). But if you try *too* hard, the visible effort only makes you look foolish.

SITUATION: You're a man; someone mentions that another man is good-looking.
STIFF: "I don't know, I guess so."
BOOR: "How would I know whether he's good-looking or not—I'm a guy!"
CHARMER: "He sure is. I'd love to look like that."

Agree with the Ridiculous

One of the best techniques for cool humor is, whenever anybody says something absurd, agree with the statement and then take it a step further. A few examples:

You're walking down the street with your prey when some crazy homeless person yells out, "The president is a faggot!" Look astonished, as if you've just had an amazing epiphany, and say wonderingly, "I never knew that. Well, come to think of it, he did go to Yale." Then add, "That's the great thing about this city. You can have a vibrant intellectual conversation with anybody you meet on the street."

If a group of criminals goes on a particularly vicious crime spree, and somebody tries to blame it on "society," nod your head sagely and say, "They had no choice."

When referring to Son of Sam, the serial killer who claimed that a dog made him do it, you might proclaim disgustedly, "Same old story. A dog tells a guy to go kill a bunch of people, and then the poor human gets all the blame."

If someone announces the earth is flat, shrug, "That's why I never go sailing. Don't want to fall off the edge."

If somebody says the moon is made of green cheese, respond, earnestly, "Somebody should look into sending an expedition to attach some ropes to that thing and drag it back to earth. We could eradicate world hunger."

Agreeing with the ridiculous is an easy technique, and it will always make you look original.

SITUATION: Someone says he thinks O. J. Simpson was innocent.

STIFF: "You really think so? But all the evidence pointed right to him!"

BOOR: "Jesus, are you a moron. He was guilty as sin—they oughta fry that fucker to a crisp."

CHARMER: (in a perfectly reasonable tone of voice) "If the glove don't fit, you must acquit."

Don't Complain

You want to be such a calm presence that your prey finds it soothing simply to be around you.

If you find yourself in a restaurant with slow service, don't go there again. But for heaven's sake, don't make it worse for your prey by carping and kvetching about it. Simply steer the conversation to more pleasant pastures, where your prey can feast on your knowledge and charm while he waits for his food to arrive.

You and your prey are looking something up on your computer, which is moving more slowly than usual. Don't complain—it'll only make the time seem to go by even more slowly. Instead, if you make interesting enough conversation, you can actually make the computer seem to work *too* fast.

You're roller-skating with your prey, and you fall and sustain a bloody cut. If it stops bleeding, just continue skating. Act as if the cut isn't even there. If your prey is used to crybabies, you'll make an impression.

SITUATION: You and your prey are stuck in the middle of a traffic jam; your car has moved exactly nine feet in the last twenty minutes.
STIFF: "This really stinks."
BOOR: Repeatedly honks his horn, although it does no good. When the driver ahead of him makes a helpless gesture, he gives him the finger and mutters darkly, "Asshole."
CHARMER: (calmly) "This would be bad, but I'm always happy to have the opportunity to spend more time with you."

If Your Prey Gets Something You Wanted

One of the best ways to get your prey to like you is to demonstrate an absolute lack of jealousy at his good fortune. If you can actually act happy for him that he has something you want, it will be doubly effective.

Let's say that you both tried out for *Jeopardy*, but only he made the cut, and is being flown out, all expenses paid, to Los Angeles for a couple days. In a situation like this, when you find out, you can't just praise your prey weakly. You must gush: "That's wonderful! I'm so happy for you, and so proud of you."

If you were rejected by med school and your prey is a prominent surgeon, swallow your pride and express happiness for his success: "All I can say is that you deserve it, you really do!"

If you can't afford the luxury apartment that your prey can, marvel, "Wow! This place is beautiful! It really is—it must be so great to live here."

This is a hard act to pull off—most of us choke on our own bile—but if you can do it, it's very impressive. And you'll probably leave your prey feeling slightly guilty about the fact that he wouldn't be nearly so magnanimous were your roles reversed.

SITUATION: Your prey has just made the final cut for the cheerleading squad and you've been cut. What do you say to her?
STIFF: "Congratulations."
BOOR: "The only reason they chose you over me is because your mom is on the school board."
CHARMER: "I'm so happy for you! I'm just so glad that at least one of us could make it!"

Keep It Clean

Nobody is ever charmed by swearing, and many people are put off by it. (When was the last time you thought to yourself, "That guy used the word 'fucking.' Wow, he's cool.")

You may have noticed that in many of the situations at the end of each chapter, the boor swears. This is not coincidence. Swearing is boorish, and swearing all the time even more so.

Here's the acid test. Think of the people you really like: how many of them swear? Then think of the people you know who swear all the time: how many of them do you really like?

Too many of us don't even hear ourselves swear. At age twelve, we may have used bad words because we weren't supposed to, and as teenagers we did it to fit in. And then the habit just stuck. But adults who swear sound either vile or juvenile.

When we're older, we sometimes swear to express either emphasis or anger. ("No fucking way" does sound a little stronger than "no way.") But if a word is used all the time, it loses its strength. And as far as insults go, how much more stinging to deliver a tailor-made barb about an opponent's sore point than the generic "Fuck you, asshole." (Refer to *The Machiavellian's Guide to Insults* for further explanation.)

Luckily, this habit is much easier to drop than, say, smoking. You needn't go into rehab, or even experience withdrawal symptoms. You simply read this chapter, then stop.

SITUATION: A giant of a man (7'2", 380 pounds) walks by.
STIFF: "Wow! Was he big!"
BOOR: (while the man is still within earshot) "God*damn*! Did you see the size of that fuck?!"
CHARMER: "All of a sudden I feel like a Lilliputian."

Afterword

No one will be able to resist your charm
if you can turn it on at the right moments.
Charm is in fact quite analyzable: it means
keeping your ego, no matter how big, in
check. At the same time, it also means
allowing your prey's to run wild. Being able to
sense when your prey is uncomfortable is
also important. If you can ease your prey's
nervousness when he is scared and help him
overcome his feelings of loneliness, he will
value your friendship and your support.
Another very useful component to charm
is the ability to recover from a faux pas, since
social errors are something we all commit.
Just having the presence of mind to mock your
own can mean coming across better than if you
had never even made them in the first place;
nobody can resist a witty self-deprecator.
Calmness is the final ingredient of charm. To
remain calm when others are waxing hysterical is
a vital part of inspiring confidence (and being cool).
If you employ the tactics in this book, you will
get your way with almost everybody.

978-0-595-47237-6
0-595-47237-0

Lightning Source UK Ltd.
Milton Keynes UK
UKOW051008030412

190063UK00001B/84/P